Springs of Wisdom

Thoughts and Moral Teachings of Āyatullāh Muḥammad Taqī Bahjat Fūmanī

AL-BURĀQ

Copyright

ISBN: 978-1-956276-31-2

Translated by The Center for Compilation and Publication of the Works of Grand Āyatullāh Bahjat.

Edited, annotated, printed, and published by al-Burāq Publications.

Where needed, context and transliterations were added. Some minor edits were made to the translated text.

Ordering Information
We offer discounts and promotions for wholesale purchases, non-profit organizations, and other educational institutions. Contact us at the email below for further information.

www.al-Buraq.org
publications@al-Buraq.org

First Edition | January 2023

Dedication

The publication of this book was made possible through the generous support of our donors.

Please recite *Sūrat al-Fātiḥah* and ask God for the Divine reward (*thawāb*) to be conferred upon the donors and also the souls of all the deceased in whose memory their loved ones have contributed graciously towards the publication of *Springs of Wisdom: Thoughts and Moral Teachings of Āyatullāh Muḥammad Taqī Bahjat Fūmanī*.

We begin by giving all praise and thanks to God عز وجل for giving us the tawfiq to translate this book. He has guided us and without Him, we would not have been guided to the straight path embodied by the Prophet Muḥammad ﷺ and the Ahl al-Bayt عليهم السلام.

This book is dedicated to all the scholars, martyrs and believers who worked tirelessly to promote the pure Muḥammadan path.

We want to also give our thanks and appreciation to all believers from around the world and acknowledge the team which helped al-Burāq Publications complete this work, spending countless hours to make its publication possible. Please recite Sūrat al-Fātiḥah on behalf of them, their families, and their marḥūmīn.

This book is dedicated in honor of the following individuals. Please remember them in your prayers and may God عز وجل have mercy on them and their loved ones.

Abrahim Ajami
Afsheen Z. Kazmi
Ali D. Saad
Ali Ftouni
Ali I. Dabaja
Alya Agemy
Amirali R. Tarbhai
Ansia Naqvi
Asgherali M. Tejani
Bande Khuda
Dia G
Feroz Naqvi
Gulshan Hudda
Hajj Ahmad Chit
Hajj Ahmad Daoud
Hajj Ali Y. Dabaja
Hajj Haidar Alaouie
Hajj Hassan Sobh
Hajj Sami Ftouni
Hajji Amneh Sobh-Ftouni
Hajji Fatme Youssef
Hajji Hiam Hojeije
Hajji Iman Elsaghir
Hajji Imane Srour
Hamid Rizvi
Hasan Kazim
Naji Mujahid
Naqi Abedi
Narjis Khatoon
Nasim A. Tejani
Nasir Hoteit
Nasrin Khan
Nawal Najdi
Pyarali Walji
Qumber K. Bhimji
Razi Zaidi
Robert Tappan
Sabiha Jafri
Sabiha Nurul H. jafri
Safaa Al Haj Hussein
Saghir Fatima
Saira Shah
Sami Saleh
Samira Alizada
Sayed Khaled M. Saleh
Sayyid A. Qadhi
Sayyid Sobh H. Sobh
Shahīd Ibrahim Hadi
Shirinbai Mithani
Sibte Haider
Syed Fidvi Ali
Syed Hussain Bokhari

Hassan M. Saleh
Hooda Jaffer
Hussein Ajrouche
Hussien Najdi
Ismael Bazzi
Janna Berry
Mahmoud Tiba
Manzur A. Tipu
Mazher Baig
Mirza Ahmed A. Baig
Mirza Mazher A. Baig
Mohamad I. Dabaja
Mohammad A. Baker
Mohammed H. Jafri
Mujahid Hussain
Syed Mehdi Ahmed
Syed Mujtaba Ahmed
Syed Nisar H. Zaidi
Syed Nurul H. Jafri
Syeda Afifa Khatoon
Syeda Amina Begum
Syeda Asghari A. Ara
Syeda Batool
Syeda Masooma Begum
Taqia Naqvi
Turfah Sobh
Wassif Hoteit
Zahra Abbas
Zahra Najdi
Zaynab Todd

Duʿāʾ al-Ḥujjah

اللهم كن لوليك الحجة بن الحسن صلواتك
عليه وعلى آبائه في هذه الساعة وفي كل
ساعة وليا وحافظا وقائدا وناصرا ودليلا
وعينا حتى تسكنه أرضك طوعا وتمتعه فيها طويلا

O God, be, for Your representative, the Ḥujjat (proof), son of al-Ḥasan, Your blessings be upon him and his forefathers, in this hour and in every hour: a guardian, a protector, a leader, a helper, a proof, and an eye—until You make him live on the Earth, in obedience (to You), and cause him to live in it for a long time.

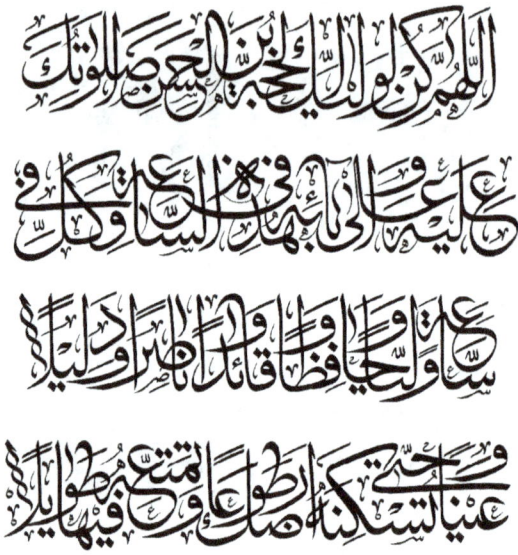

Terms of Respect

The following Arabic phrases have been used throughout this book in their respective places to show the reverence which the noble personalities deserve.

عَزَّ وَجَلَّ

Used for God, meaning:
Exalted and Sublime (Perfect) is He

صَلَّى اللهُ عَلَيْهِ وَآلِهِ

Used for Prophet Muḥammad, meaning:
Blessings from God be upon him and his family

عَلَيْهِ السَّلَامُ

Used for a man (singular) of a high status, meaning:
Peace be upon him

عَلَيْهَا السَّلَامُ

Used for a woman (singular) of a high status, meaning:
Peace be upon her

عَلَيْهِمَا السَّلَامُ

Used for men/women (dual) of a high status, meaning:
Peace be upon them both

عَلَيْهِمُ السَّلَامُ

Used for men and/or women (plural) of a high status, meaning:
Peace be upon them all

عَجَّلَ اللهُ تَعَالَى فَرَجَهُ الشَّرِيفَ

Used for Imām Muḥammad al-Mahdī, meaning:
May God hasten his return

قُدِّسَ سِرُّهُ

Used for a deceased scholar, meaning:
May his resting [burial] place remain pure

Transliteration Table

The method of transliteration of Islamic terminology from the Arabic language has been carried out according to the standard transliteration table below.

ء	ʾ	ر	r	ف	f
ا	a	ز	z	ق	q
ب	b	س	s	ك	k
ت	t	ش	sh	ل	l
ث	th	ص	ṣ	م	m
ج	j	ض	ḍ	ن	n
ح	ḥ	ط	ṭ	و	w
خ	kh	ظ	ẓ	ه	h
د	d	ع	ʿ	ي	y
ذ	dh	غ	gh		
Long Vowels					
ا	ā	و	ū	ي	ī
Short Vowels					
ــَـ	a	ــُـ	u	ــِـ	i

Table of Contents

Translator's Notes

بسم الله الرحمن الرحيم

In the Name of God, the Beneficent, the Merciful

It has been an honor and a pleasure to help in translating this precious book of short sayings from Āyatullāh Bahjat, a précis of 80 years of experience and studies of a man that spent his life in an intellectual and practical journey towards God Almighty, a unique personality who was renowned as a Marjaʿ in Shīʿa jurisprudence, a great mystic in spiritual wayfaring, and a knowledgeable scholar in Qur'ān and aḥādīth (Islamic Narrations).

Among his well-known characteristics was that he talked very little. His short sayings that were full of wisdom and were derived from verses of the Qur'ān, aḥādīth and his spiritual experiences are springs of wisdom.

I tried to maintain the spirit of the words in the translation while making it understandable for English speakers, despite its difficulty, because of the language of the Āyatullāh, which is hard to understand in Farsi, let alone in English. For instance, he says, "God knows best the state of those who have spiritual stations at the time of supplication and solitude; and how the silence of pondering burns them as a result of witnessing the divine lights, even if for a short duration." It is hard to understand what silence of pondering means, therefore, if there is any hardship in the understanding of the words, it is because of the language he used, rather than the accuracy of translation.

There were a few words that I had slight trouble translating, and these words were commonly used by Āyatullāh Bahjat. One was the word '*bala*' and another similar word, '*ibtila*'. I translated both as 'afflictions', which is not perfect, but it distinguishes both from plight. Another word that was used quite often by the Āyatullāh is '*tawfeeq*', which implies the ability and opportunity to fulfill a task, but since this ability and opportunity comes from God Almighty, I translated it as 'Divine Assistance'. '*Muraqabah*' is originally an Arabic word which means 'to watch over', 'to take care of', or 'to keep an eye' which I translated as 'attentive observation' since, in Islamic Mysticism, it is more than just taking care of something.

It is obvious that spreading the words of great Shi'a scholars who are drowned in the Book and Sunnah of the Prophet, is in reality, spreading the school and words of the Ahl al-Bayt عليهم السلام. The mysticism that Āyatullāh Bahjat practiced is pure Shīʿa Mysticism and is in accordance with the school of Ahl al-Bayt peace be upon them; and this is the mysticism that is approved and worthy of being followed.

Morteza Namazi

March 15, 2016

Qom, Iran

Biography of Āyatullāh Bahjat

His Childhood

On the night of the 25th of Shawwal 1334 A.H (August 23, 1916) the home of Karbalā'ī Mahmūd was blessed with the birth of a child that later went on to win the hearts of millions of lovers of knowledge and truth amongst the Shī'a of the infallible household of the Prophet, peace be upon him and his pure progeny. He came to be known as Āyatullāh Hajj Shaykh Muḥammad Taqī Bahjat ﷺ.

The righteous, well-known and trustworthy Karbalā'ī Mahmūd from Fūman, in the province of Gīlān, named his new son Muḥammad Taqī, inspired by an event in his youth.[1]

His mother's death was the first tragic incident in his life. Muḥammad Taqī had seen his mother's affection for only 16 months, and her death saddened all. His older sister played the role of his mother from then on.

From his childhood, Muḥammad Taqī had been in his father's loving company and he would see the enthusiasm for Ahl al-Bayt ﷺ emit from his father's heart, put to paper and used as eulogies by the bereaved mourners of Imām al-Ḥusayn ﷺ.

---

[1] The elders of the town narrate that when Karbalā'ī Maḥmūd was suffering from cholera at the age of 17 or 18 and on the verge of death, he heard a voice in his sleep, saying, "Let him go, he is Muḥammad Taqī's father." He recovered soon after.

During those times, Muḥammad Taqī, whilst in his father's loving company even at this very tender age, composed eulogies himself. He was attracted to this martyr of love and grief, and his oppressed Imām was placed in his heart from then until the end of his life.[2]

The mourning ceremonies of Imām al-Ḥusayn ﷺ from every corner of the city, turned Muḥammad Taqī's attention towards the traditional school of Mullah Ḥusayn Koʿkabi Fūmani, and placed him amongst the reciters of the holy verses of the noble Qur'ān.

In the peace and quiet of his surroundings, he was acquainted with the pleasurable call of '*a*l-ḥamdu li-llāhi rabbi l-ʿālamīn*a*'

(All praise be to God, Lord of the Worlds) and gave his tongue the fragrance of the verses of the Noble Qur'ān, enthusiastically memorizing some chapters of it.

However, his thirsty soul could not be quenched, and he made his way to the Islamic seminary of Fūman so that the verses of the Noble Qur'ān, and the teachings of the pure Imāms, peace be upon them, could further soothe the ears of his soul.

---

[2] Imām Jaʿfar al-Ṣādiq ﷺ has said, "Verily the Martyrdom of Imām al-Ḥusayn has put a fire in the believers hearts that will never be quenched."

In Fūman's lively Islamic seminary where varieties of religious sciences were discussed, he met Āyatullāh 'Aḥmad Sa'idi Fūmanī, self-purified, a great man of piety and knowledge, a person he greatly benefited from and with an ineffable seriousness and insatiable spirit, he quickly learned Islamic sciences along with a few Persian texts such as the *Bustan* (The Orchard), *Golestan* (The Rosary) and *Kelileh va Demneh,* and after seven years of continuous efforts, he was ranked among the top students of his master. Blissful moments during the congregational prayers led by Āyatullāh Fūmanī, were remembered by both him and his student.[3]

In Jumāda al-Thāni of the year 1348, coinciding with November 1929, it was time for Muḥammad Taqī to migrate from home. Undoubtedly, the mentioning of the glorious Islamic seminaries of Iraq during the solitary moments that Muḥammad Taqī had with the scholars of Fūman's seminary, who themselves had been educated in Najaf, exhilarated his eagerness, and took his heart to the shining domes of the Holy Shrine of Imām 'Alī and Imām al-Ḥusayn عليهما السلام.

Setting off to Iraq

Muḥammad Taqī decided to migrate to Iraq, longing to calm his restless soul at the shrine of the infallible

[3] For years, Āyatullāh Sa'idi Fūmanī inquired about Āyatullāh Bahjat from his father, asking "How is our classmate?"

Imāms, and quench his thirst for truth in the presence of great scholars of the Islamic seminary of Iraq.

Having seen his enthusiasm, his father sent him to Karbalā with one of his well-to-do friends. On his first trip, Muḥammad Taqī failed to leave the country. The border police did not allow him to enter Iraq because of the absence of his parents. Although disappointed, remembering a childhood incident made him certain that he would go to Karbalā. He later did so… kissing the shrine of Imām al-Ḥusayn عليه السلام and smelling the blessed soil of Karbalā.

At that time, Muḥammad Taqī was around fourteen years of age and had gained an abundance of knowledge even before having reached the religious age of puberty.

Muḥammad Taqī stayed with his uncle who was living in Iraq at that time, and after about a year, he moved to the seminary dorm and attended school. The Islamic Seminary of Karbalā was filled with great scholars. During that year, Muḥammad Taqī studied parts of Islamic jurisprudence (Fīqh) and basic principles of jurisprudence (Uṣūl) and in his second year, he put on the sacred clerical robe in the presence of Āyatullāh Ja'far Ḥā'irī Fūmanī and his father, who joined him in Karbalā.

He spent four years in Karbalā and with continuous efforts, acquired knowledge, and insight, along with self-purification, and achieved excellence in ethics under the blessed shrine of the Master of Martyrs عليه السلام. Undoubtedly, the precious moments on the threshold of the Martyr of Love were far greater than the hours spent in search of knowledge.

Migrating to Najaf

It was time to leave the Islamic Seminary of Karbalā for the Islamic Seminary of Najaf, home, and the holy shrine of the Commander of the Faithful عليه السلام.

Najaf's renowned seminary, with a history of one thousand years, was home to many theosophists, men of knowledge and piety. A place of mystics for those in search.

Āyatullāh Muḥammad Taqī strived with determination and courage, seeking the knowledge entrusted by the Ahl al-Bayt عليهم السلام in the Islamic Seminary of Najaf. He completed the advanced Islamic sciences with Āyatullāh Murtaḍā Tāleqānī, Sayyid Hādī Mīlānī, Āyatullāh Sayyid Abū al-Qāsim Khū'ī, Āyatullāh 'Alī Muḥammad Burūjirdī and Āyatullāh Sayyid Mahmoud Shāhroudī . He then began to study the advanced Principles of Jurisprudence (*Kharej-e Uṣūl*) and advanced Islamic Jurisprudence (*Kharej –e Fīqh*).

To study these advanced lessons he sat on the footstool of teachers of Islamic Jurisprudence (Fīqh), Principles of Jurisprudence (Uṣūl) and Insight of Ahl al-Bayt.

His favorite teachers included Āyatullāh Ḍiya ʿIrāqi, Āyatullāh Mīrzāye Moʿīnī and Āyatullāh Muḥammad Kāẓim Shīrāzī.

He also benefited greatly from the distinguished scholar, Āyatullāh Sayyid Abu al-Ḥasan al-Isfahānī in Islamic Jurisprudence (Fīqh).

Āyatullāh Muḥammad Taqī's creativity, intellect, and meticulous attention to his studies made him a renowned student, whose questions were regarded seriously by his professors.[4]

Besides Uṣūl and Fīqh, Āyatullāh Muḥammad Taqī was interested in philosophy and rational sciences, for which he studied the books *al-Ishārāt wal Tanbīhāt* and *Isfār* with Āyatullāh Sayyid Ḥusayn Badkubi.

Teaching advanced Islamic sciences at the seminary, and assisting the great Shaykh ʿAbbās Qummī (compiler of

[4] To honor his master Āyatullāh Muḥammad-Ḥusayn Na'ini ﵀, he said, "Before I became of religious age, I attended his congregational prayer and experienced such a state that I had experienced only in the congregational prayers of Āyatullāh Saʿidi Fūmani.

Mafātīḥ al-Jinān) to compile the book *Safīnat al-Biḥār* were amongst his other activities.

This, however, was not all that he gained from the great scholars of Najaf's seminary. He attained new spiritual heights and mystical knowledge alongside his masters in 'Irfan.[5]

He was deeply influenced by two prominent figures, the first being the great scholar Āyatullāh Gharawī Isfahānī, also known as '*Kumpānī*', who possessed a genius methodical and philosophic mind. In addition to the methodical lessons of his master, Āyatullāh Bahjat gained spiritual and ethical benefits, which became a part of his character. The second figure that left a great impact on Āyatullāh Bahjat was a unique mystic ('ārif) and seeker of knowledge, Āyatullāh Mīrzā 'Alī Qāḍī, قدس سره.

When Āyatullāh Muḥammad Taqī entered Najaf at the age of 18, he found the teacher he was in search of in Āyatullāh Mīrzā Qāḍī—a mountain of Tawḥīd (monotheism) in the words of Āyatullāh Sayyid Khumaynī.

---

[5] The late 'Allamah Muḥammad Taqī Ja'fari قدس سره says, "When I was a student of Agha Āyatullāh Kāẓim Shīrāzī studying advanced Makāsib, Āyatullāh Bahjat was in the same class. I remember well that whenever he raised a question Āyatullāh Kāẓim paid close attention to it.

Although very young, he managed to finish the itinerary of the spiritual path and become the pride of others, and attract his master's close attention. He was called the scholar of Gīlān.[6]

The peaks and valleys of life in Najaf al-Ashraf provided him with a golden opportunity for self-purification and self-discipline, but the burden of his studies and his endeavor in purification and self-discipline was such that he became ill. He would treat himself by traveling to Samarra, Kāẓimiya and Karbalā under different weather conditions.

After sixteen years of living near the shining dome of the Commander of the Faithful, Imām 'Alī ☙, and the Master of the Martyrs, Imām al-Ḥusayn ☙, with an untiring determination to acquire knowledge and insight in the presence of the best Islamic scholars that the seminary had to offer, Muḥammad Taqī reached the stage of Ijtihād and returned home to Fūman.

In Jumāda al-Thānī of the year 1364 Hijri, coinciding with August 1945, after having reached the age of 30, on his sister's advice, he decided to get married.

---

[6] A part of the letter sent to his student Ilahī Tabātabā'ī by Āyatullāh Qāḍī reads, "Agha Āyatullāh Muḥammad Taqī Gīlānī has made great progress in his studies."

After a few months in Fūman, Āyatullāh Bahjat decided to travel to Najaf after the month of Ramadan of that year. He decided to stop by in Qom to get his passport and acquire information about the Islamic Seminary of Qom before continuing towards Najaf.

The Holiest Shrine of the Ahl al-Bayt عليهم السلام

In the month of Shawwal 1364 A.H, coinciding with September 1945, Āyatullāh Bahjat set off for Qom. During his temporary stay in Qom, he received a series of heartbreaking news. On 28th of Safar, a few months into his stay in Qom, he received the news of his father's passing. However, he took comfort in the knowledge that his father was happy and content with the path his son had chosen before he left this world. Then followed from Najaf the news of the demise of Āyatullāh Abu al-Ḥasan al-Isfahānī and Āyatullāh Mīrzā ʿAlī Qāḍī in Najaf, both of whom were revered and dearly loved by him.

These were two of his masters that he had the fondest memories of from Najaf. This news was one of the reasons he lost his will to go back to Najaf and decided to stay permanently in Qom, near the blessed shrine of the Ahl al-Bayt عليهم السلام and the Islamic Seminary.

Agha Bahjat's presence in the holy city of Qom had an outstanding impact on his life as well as the lives of many others.

He attended the advanced classes of the Marājiʿ (Great Scholars) in Qom. After 24 years of its revival by Āyatullāh Ḥā'irī, the Islamic seminary of Qom had become a powerful seminary with the presence of distinguished scholars and mujtahids. Although Āyatullāh Bahjat was a mujtahid of the highest standard, he, along with Āyatullāh Sayyid Khumaynī, Āyatullāh Gulpāyigānī and a few others, attended the classes of Āyatullāh Sayyid Ḥusayn Burūjirdī and Āyatullāh Muḥammad Ḥujjat Kūh Kamarī out of respect to the elders of the seminary. He was among the best students of his masters and became one of the most important critics of the class.

At the same time, he would also teach Uṣūl and Fīqh that lasted for over 60 years, right to the end of his blessed life.

In the mornings, he would teach advanced jurisprudence (Khareje Fīqh) and in the afternoons, he would teach advanced principles (Khareje Uṣūl). To avoid publicity, he first chose to teach in seminary rooms, and then moved the lessons to his home. Later on, in 1398 Hijri (1978 AD), at the insistence of his students, he moved the lessons to the Fāṭimīyya Mosque, where he taught for the rest of his life.

His regular Friday morning ceremony of Imām al-Ḥusayn عليه السلام was first held at his house and then was moved to the Fāṭimīyya Mosque. Through heat and cold, health and sickness, he continued to attend the Mourning sessions of Imām al-Ḥusayn ﷺ until the end of his life. He would spend a part of the summer in Mashhad and these ceremonies would be held there during his stay. His insistence on having these weekly sessions was due to the will and recommendation of his beloved teacher of ethics, Āyatullāh Mīrzā Qāḍī, who would say, "Do not forget the weekly Friday ceremonies of Imām al-Ḥusayn."[7]

He would lead all daily prayers in the congregation, which included the attendance of many great-distinguished scholars that were prominent personalities in their own right. In the last years of his life, he would only lead the afternoon prayers due to sickness. The feeling one would have during these prayers could not be expressed in words and could only be understood by some of those who were among the crowded lines that stretched from the mosque to the alley outside the mosque, listening to his prayer recitation.

He continued his daily morning ziyāra (visitation) to the Holy Shrine of Lady Maʿsūma ﷺ, the sister of Imām ʿAlī al-Riḍā ﷺ, after the morning prayers and duʿāʾs until the end of his blessed life at around the age

[7] Part of the will of Āyatullāh Mīrzā Qāḍī ﷺ to Āyatullāh Bahjat read, "Do not neglect holding the weekly mourning sessions of the Master of Martyrs. It will help ease the pain."

of 90. He would sit in a corner of the holy shrine and recite ziyāra and du'ā'.

Āyatullāh Bahjat also wrote books on Uṣūl and Fīqh but did not have them published. He did not permit others to publish them even with their own money, saying, "There are still many manuscripts of great scholars that need to be published first."

Some of his books include: 'Mabaheth al-Uṣūl', 'A Commentary and Review of Shaykh Anṣārī's Makāsib', and completed the book until the chapter of business (*Mu'āmalāt*), '*Bahjat al-Faqihiyeh*', Book review of *Zakhirat al-Ebad*, Book review of Shaykh Anṣārī's *Manasek*, along with books of couplets and poems.

Major books that have been published by the insistence of his students include the '*Risalay Tozih al-Masā'il*' in Persian and Arabic, and '*Rites of Hajj*'. These two books were published by a group of scholars that compiled his *Fatwas* with his approval. One of his other books is his commentary on the book '*Vasilat al-Nejat*', written by his master, Āyatullāh Sayyid Abu al-Ḥasan al-Isfahānī. The first volume of this book had been published with his approval. There is also the '*Jam'i al-Masā'il*', a course on *Fatwas* in Islamic Jurisprudence, which was the result of 25 years of expertise in the field. This invaluable book came out in 1992 in five volumes.

His diligence and efforts for over half a century cannot be put into words. It is impossible to express the feeling of his followers through simple words when the biggest impact he had on others was through other than words. Expressing the new feelings in the state of worship goes beyond the scope of this brief biography. How can one introduce the students that spread out like branches of a tree in every direction, attempting to elaborate upon a part of his teachings? Words cannot describe the prayer lines whose breaths were taken away by one of his mystic sighs.

Illustrious

Undoubtedly, one of the outstanding characteristics of Āyatullāh Bahjat was his tendency to shun publicity and insistently attempt to remain anonymous. In his younger days, when he realized that his insightful questions in classes of the great Maraji' were giving him publicity, he stopped asking them. He did not insist on teaching either. That is why he never chose a fixed suitable place to teach. His attendance in the classes of Āyatullāh al-Burūjirdī and other scholars at a time when he was well capable of teaching the same courses was another proof of his humility and anonymity.

Although he was one of the best students of Āyatullāh Mīrzā Qāḍī and acquired spiritual blessings in his childhood, he never promoted himself, and always refused to talk about the mystical experiences he gained in the company of his masters.[8]

When he would speak of his masters, he had to reveal some of his own secrets, but he never used the word 'I' while speaking.

He also never had any ambitions to become a Marjaʿ Taqlīd (religious authority). Even with 45 years of experience teaching advanced Principles and Islamic Jurisprudence, he refused to accept this position.

Nevertheless, after the demise of Āyatullāh Sayyid ʾAḥmad Khwānsārī and Sayyid Abū al-Qāsim Khū'ī, a large number of believers, as well as many scholars, pressed upon him to publish his Risāla. He accepted their request, but with the condition that the book should not have his name on the cover.[9]

It is obvious that this great man, who had devoted his entire life to God ﷻ, earned a lofty position in the eyes of his Lord, in return for his sincerity in worship and

---

[8] One of his students relates that "In all the years I have been attending his class, I have never heard him talk about himself."

[9] One of his close relatives was quoted as saying, "Before the demise of Āyatullāh Arākī, when Āyatullāh Bahjat realized that the Seniors of the Hawza were going to introduce him as a religious authority, he sent a message showing his dissatisfaction with the announcement of his name."

servitude to his creator, and by the will of God عزّ وجلّ, he won the hearts of millions of believers around the world without intending to do so. How can words describe this special servant of God عزّ وجلّ who won hearts by the heart, not by words!

Looking Forward to the Union...

The midst of May 2009 were the last days of his waiting. During his entire blessed life, and now with a fatigued fragile body and thirst-filled soul, he wished to unite with the eternal. Someone who was a righteous servant of God عزّ وجلّ and thought of nothing other than being a good servant of his creator all his life, the moment of leaving for his beloved was the height of all joys for this true 'ārif (Gnostic). The ninety years of spiritual and physical struggle culminated with a secure and loving embrace by his Lord. However, his peace and tranquility was for his followers, lovers and students, an endless sorrow and grief. Devastated, they came in masses to see, for one last time, his blessed luminous face busy in the remembrance of God.

Sunday, the evening of the 17th of May 2009 was indeed, a sad evening for Qom. When the news of the demise of this great religious scholar broke out, it spread everywhere quickly. At first, all were in shock, and then the whole city was in mourning. Once the news was announced by the news agencies, devoted followers from all over the country rushed to Qom. On that day,

Qom was covered in black. Since Āyatullāh Burūjirdī's funeral, Qom had never witnessed such enormous crowds of people for a funeral ceremony.

The body of this old sage and mystic was put to rest in the Holy Shrine of Lady Fāṭimah Maʿsūma.

Now the silence of the Fāṭimīyyah Mosque is the cry of separation. Now the small wooden door near the window beside the altar, his lovers and followers' hearts can only imagine an old man walking through the door with his face turned down, his lips fragrant with the remembrance of God ﷻ, his eyes wet with tears and his forehead illuminated by the effects of prostration.

In the solitude of this mosque if you now desire seclusion, you must turn your head and lend the ears of your heart to the holy shrine of Ahl al-Bayt عليهم السلام to listen to the recitation of Sūrat al-Fātiḥah and Sūrat al-Ikhlāṣ.

Maybe once again the call of Yasin Wal Qur'ān al-Hakim of the Fāṭimīyya Mosque will enter the divine realm of Friday mornings, but his seat will only be occupied by his soul.

Āyatullāh Bahjat in the Words of Islamic Scholars

Āyatullāh Sayyid Khumaynī

Āyatullāh Sayyid Khumaynī used to pay special attention to Āyatullāh Bahjat, as is evident from the following incidents.

Āyatullāh Masoudi says, "During the four or five years when I was serving Āyatullāh Sayyid Khumaynī, I remember that he said to me two or three times: We will go to the house of Āyatullāh Bahjat tomorrow, so be prepared for it. The next day, we went to the house of the Āyatullāh and sat in the first room, which was then carpeted with the same carpet that has always been there. Āyatullāh Sayyid Khumaynī asked me to go out. I went out of the house whilst he stayed behind talking to Āyatullāh Bahjat for about half an hour. He then came out of the house and we returned together. As for the subject of their discussion, I have no knowledge of it – only God knows."

"Sometimes during the days of revolution (the years 1963 and 1964), Āyatullāh Bahjat would say to me, "Ask Sayyid Khumaynī to slaughter two sheep tomorrow morning at such an hour seeking nearness to God Almighty." I would go to Āyatullāh Sayyid Khumaynī and tell him so, and he would say,"Ask the butcher to slaughter two sheep on our account, and I shall pay him later." Once Āyatullāh Bahjat said to me, "Tell Āyatullāh Sayyid Khumaynī to slaughter three sheep."

He then ordered three sheep to be slaughtered. All these matters used to go on between him and Āyatullāh Bahjat; we would be witnessing them outwardly, whilst having no knowledge of what they implied."

"When Āyatullāh Sayyid Khumaynī was residing in Jamaran, Āyatullāh Bahjat once said to me, "I have a small letter that I would like you to deliver to him." I took the letter from him, put it in an envelope, and delivered it to Āyatullāh Sayyid Khumaynī. The relationship between Āyatullāh Bahjat and Āyatullāh Sayyid Khumaynī was very strong."

Āyatullāh Miṣbāḥ Yazdī قدس سره says the following in this regard elsewhere, "The late Sayyid Muṣṭafā (may God be pleased with him) says about his late father Āyatullāh Sayyid Khumaynī قدس سره that when he saw the simplicity of Āyatullāh Bahjat's life, he took a sum of money from Sayyid Burūjirdī (with whom he had strong ties) in order to give it to Āyatullāh Bahjat, but Sayyid Burūjirdī refused to accept this sum. On the other hand, Āyatullāh Sayyid Khumaynī did not see any benefit in returning this sum to Sayyid Burūjirdī therefore, he had to think of a way to tackle this issue. He therefore said to Āyatullāh Bahjat, "I give you a grant from my own money, and forgive me for not returning this sum." Thus Āyatullāh Bahjat accepted the sum as a grant from Āyatullāh Sayyid Khumaynī own money'."

Āyatullāh Miṣbāḥ says the following referring to the special attention that the late Āyatullāh Sayyid Khumaynī would give to Āyatullāh Bahjat. "Once the Assembly of Experts were honored to visit the late Āyatullāh Sayyid Khumaynī. They asked him for instructions on ethical issues, so he referred them to the Āyatullāh Bahjat. They said to him, "But he does not accept anyone." Āyatullāh Sayyid Khumaynī said, "Keep insisting until he accepts."

Āyatullāh Sayyid ʿAlī Ḥusaynī Khāminaʾī

That noble man, who was considered as one of the most outstanding contemporary jurists, was also a great teacher of ethics, spirituality, and the spring of endless, spiritual blessings. The pure heart of this devout individual was a mirror, polished by Divine Revelation, and his words were a guide for the thoughts and actions of the wayfarers.

Āyatullāh Muḥammad Kāẓim Shīrāzī

Āyatullāh Maḥfūzi told the writer, "Once when we were members of the Supreme Council of the Islamic Seminary, we came to meet Āyatullāh Mūsā Zanjānī. After the meeting, in the courtyard of his house, I asked him how he would describe Āyatullāh Bahjat. He said, "Two things:

1. We would attend his lectures and we found him very precise; he would discuss his topics like a researcher.

2. The late Āyatullāh Muḥammad Kāẓim Shīrāzī, who had come to Qom from Najaf, said in the house of the late Sayyid Muḥammad Ruhani, "Do not be heedless of Āyatullāh Muḥammad Taqī; he has worked very hard in Najaf."

Āyatullāh Sayyid ʿAlī Ḥusaynī Sīstānī

The loss of this noble man, who was one of the giant scholars, and enjoyed a great spiritual station, is indeed a huge loss.

Āyatullāh Jawādi Amoli

We would often tell ʿAllamah, "Give us a class on ethics; we want to benefit." He would reply, "Ethics cannot be said, they are to be acted. Look at Agha Bahjat, his entire life is a class on ethics; his coming, and going, and meeting people, all of it is a class on ethics."

ʿAllamah Tabātabāʾī

ʿAllamah Tabātabāʾī said, "Āyatullāh Bahjat is a true and righteous servant of God."

Āyatullāh Bahā' al-Dīnī

Āyatullāh Bahā' al-Dīnī said, "Āyatullāh Bahjat is regarded as the richest man in the world (spiritually)."

Āyatullāh Fakour

Āyatullāh Muḥammad Ḥasan al-Aḥmadī said, "Āyatullāh Fakour used to pay special attention to Āyatullāh Bahjat; he used to say, "Āyatullāh Bahjat is an exceptional individual, especially in spiritual matters."

Āyatullāh Sayyid 'Abd al-Karīm Kashmīrī

Sayyid Kashmīrī was asked once about the person whom he knew as a perfect mentor. He said, "It is Shaykh Bahjat, Shaykh Bahjat."

Sayyid Fahri

Sayyid Fahri too, was asked, "Who is the person that you know is a perfect mentor?" He said, "It is Āyatullāh Bahjat, Āyatullāh Bahjat."

Āyatullāh 'Abbās Qouchānī

Āyatullāh Miṣbāḥ Yazdī says, "Amongst the individuals that believed that Āyatullāh Bahjat enjoyed lofty spiritual perfections is Āyatullāh 'Abbās Qouchānī, the student of the late Sayyid ʿAlī Qāḍī, who lived in the city of Najaf. He used to say, "Even before turning twenty, Āyatullāh Bahjat had already attained lofty stations, which I realized because of our friendship. The Āyatullāh took a Sharʿī pledge from me that I would not narrate any of it to anyone." I think he meant 'death by choice.' Āyatullāh Bahjat had attained these stations in such a young age, and you can imagine his station in nearness to God Almighty at the age of eighty, after a long age of conduct and straightforwardness in adoration and in acting upon the obligations. It is for this reason that every good believer feels attracted to him upon seeing him, especially when he sees his worship. Let people offer their prayers behind him if God gives them the chance to do so, for there are many blessings in it."

Āyatullāh Mishkīnī

Āyatullāh Mishkīnī said, "Āyatullāh Bahjat occupies a very lofty station among Shīʿa scholars from the scholarly standpoint in Fīqh and Uṣūl. Likewise, his students have a very lofty station; so much so, that we must look upon them as we look at the stars in the sky. Therefore, writing books on the dimensions of the personality of Āyatullāh Bahjat is a must."

ʿAllamah Muḥammad Taqī Jaʿfari

ʿAllamah Jaʿfari said, "Traditions state that if one does not visit a scholar for forty days, his heart dies. Visiting scholars is more beloved to God ﷻ than circling the Kaʿbah seventy times. Āyatullāh Bahjat is one true example of the scholars mentioned in these traditions. One is truly admonished by looking at him and visiting him. Whenever I meet him, the effect of the meeting lingers in my soul for several days. Indeed, he is a warner to us."

Āyatullāh Miṣbāḥ Yazdī

Āyatullāh Miṣbāḥ Yazdī said, "Āyatullāh Bahjat incorporated in himself the precisions of the late Mīrzā Muḥammad Taqī Shīrāzī through his prominent students, such as Āyatullāh Muḥammad Kāẓim. He also summed up the excellences of the late Na'īnī and the late Āyatullāh Muḥammad Ḥusayn Isfahānī, as well as spiritual training of the late Qāḍī. These professors brought up an inclusive personality, which is regarded as one of the greatest blessings of our time. It is possible to benefit even from the small moments of his lifetime. God ﷻ bestowed special distinctions and self-gifts upon Āyatullāh Bahjat, which he did not acquire from anyone, and he, despite all of this, concealed his spiritual stations, not permitting those who were aware of it to mention them anywhere. Āyatullāh Bahjat also took care of scholarly matters, dealing with them with precision. He used to think that a class is an obligation, something serious, and he used to give special attention to matters of Fīqh. He was extremely interested in worship and moral issues, believing that they are the second wing of man's ascension and perfection."

Āyatullāh Ṭāhirī Shams

Āyatullāh Ṭāhirī Shams said, "Āyatullāh Bahjat reached a lofty level and a sublime horizon (in Fīqh), so much so, that if he looked at rulings and Islamic legislations, he would be able to derive a fatwa that pleases God ﷻ, and there is no dispute in this."

Āyatullāh Jawād Karbalā'ī

Āyatullāh Jawād Karbalā'ī said, "During my stay in Tehran and Qom in these years, I heard from some people which indicated that Āyatullāh Bahjat enjoyed special divine niceties; so congratulations to him, then congratulations again to him."

Āyatullāh Azari Qomi

Āyatullāh Azari Qomi said, " Āyatullāh Bahjat is regarded as one of the students of Āyatullāh Na'īnī and Āyatullāh Isfahānī; he has valuable findings in teachings. Virtuous men of the Islamic Seminary in Qom, who attended his classes for more than fifteen years, became skillful Mujtahids. Āyatullāh Bahjat was famous for his piety and godliness in the holy city of Qom, in addition to his academic fame, which was known throughout the world. As some brethren say, it cannot be said that Āyatullāh Bahjat was just pious; rather, he is piety itself. Piety and equity are the best qualities with which the authorities for Taqlīd are characterized. Āyatullāh Bahjat was characterized by these two qualities, personifying them in his own self."

Āyatullāh Masʿūdī Khumaynī

Āyatullāh Masʿūdī Khumaynī said, "Very few are the likes of Āyatullāh Bahjat in all ages; therefore, we must benefit from him in the best way, especially because he has achieved a lofty degree in morals and ethics. Let everyone, especially the youths, and those seeking spirituality, go to him in order to learn their lessons from him, because his existence personifies spirituality and manners. Even looking at his face has innumerable ethical and moral benefits."

Ḥujjatul Islām Fīqhi

Ḥujjatul Islām Fīqhi said, "If the tree of humanity produced another good fruit, other than the Infallibles, peace be upon them, one such fruit is his Excellency, Āyatullāh Bahjat."

Āyatullāh Muḥammad Ḥusayn Aḥmadi Faqih

Āyatullāh Muḥammad Ḥusayn Aḥmadi Faqih from Yazd said, "We are certain that Āyatullāh Bahjat will be one of the pilgrims of God on the Day of Judgment. If we fail to benefit from his lectures properly, it will be held against us, and we shall have no answer when asked by our Lord."

Ḥujjatul Islām ʾAmjad

Ḥujjatul Islām Amjad said, "Āyatullāh Bahjat is regarded as one of the prides of the scholars of our time. Anyone who knows him, in one way or another, knows that he acquired a lofty station on account of his knowledge and spirituality. I think there is no peer for him in knowledge and spirituality. In other words, he is an angel living on earth. We, therefore, must benefit from the blessings of his presence."

Ḥujjatul Islām Khosro Shāhi

It is not possible for one to recognize Āyatullāh Bahjat and his levels of perfection except through self-purification and increasing one's existential capacity, and everyone can understand him in accordance with the vastness of his own existential capacity. Based on this, in order to recognize his perfections, one must carry out self-purification and expand his existential capacity in order to be able to benefit more from his perfections.

Short Sayings

Manifestations of Monotheism and Divine Knowledge

1. Reality of the Dhikr of God

Invocating God ﷻ (dhikr), which has no limits, consists of dhikr with the heart and tongue, as well as bodily dhikr, because all religious obligations, and all that pleases God ﷻ are dhikr of God ﷻ.

2. Divine Assistance from the Sustainer

There should be divine help and assistance from God ﷻ so that voluntary deeds are carried out with the choice and will of man.

3. Describing Heaven and Hell

God ﷻ has elevated Heaven and its dwellers so much in His ﷻ descriptions of them in the Noble Qur'ān other texts that it would not be unlikely for one to die because of the pleasure of listening to it. The verses regarding hell are similar... It would not be unlikely for one to think about his sins and die.

4. The Real Beloved

Is it good to be friends with, and turn to one in whose hands is our life and death, health and illness, wealth and poverty, or one who himself is dependent, weak, and helpless?

5. Greatest Worship

The cognizance of God is the greatest of worship and all religious rituals are a preliminary to His ﷻ cognizance.

6. Meaning of Teaching the Names

﴿وَعَلَّمَ آدَمَ الأَسماءَ كُلَّها﴾

﴿*wa-ʿallama ʾādama l-ʾasmāʾa kullahā*﴾

﴿*And He taught Adam the Names, all of them;*﴾[10]

The purport of this verse is that the knowledge of those realities becomes the cause of man's distinction over animals, rather, the angels.

7. Purpose of Creation

The consequence of creation and the creature in the Ḥadīth Qudsi: "[O Muḥammad] I have created all things for you and you for myself" is knowledge and [Divine] Cognizance.

---

[10] Sūrat al-Baqarah, Verse 31.

It is to be noted that the pronoun in 'all of them' [*kullahā*] is feminine.

8. Angels Recording our Words

Angels record our voices, and they record both our words, as well as if they have been uttered with a divine motive, or with a carnal and satanic purpose.

9. Relationship of This World with the Hereafter

The relationship of this world with the hereafter is like that of a mother's womb with this world; death is the birth of the soul.

At the Doorstep of the Prophet's عليهم السلام Household

10. Worship of the Infallibles

The Holy Infallibles عليهم السلام both feared hell, and desired heaven, but they did not worship out of their fear and desires.

11. Recognize the Imām to Recognize God

If the recognition of Imām Muḥammad al-Mahdī عجل الله تعالى فرجه الشريف increases, recognition of God عز وجل will also increase, for is there any sign greater than the Imām عجل الله تعالى فرجه الشريف? The Imām عجل الله تعالى فرجه الشريف is the mirror that reflects the realities of the entire universe.

12. The Imāms are not Heedless of us

The Imāms عليهم السلام are never heedless of our states, even though we may be heedless of them.

13. Reason Behind Afflictions

Every affliction that we encounter is the result of our distance from Ahl al-Bayt عليهم السلام and their authentic narrations.

14. Sensing the Presence of Ahl al-Bayt

Salvation is for one who sees Ahl al-Bayt عليهم السلام present and the addressee everywhere.

15. How Should We Be?

Follow in the footsteps of the Infallibles عليهم السلام, not in the footsteps of others! Stay with ʿUlamāʾ (Islamic Scholars), always be well informed, and be concerned with useful, life-inspiring information.

16. Divine Assistance for Ziyāra

The blessing of performing ziyāra has nothing to do with having money.

17. Responsibility of Iranians

Iranians must value the blessing of the Holy Shrine of Imām ʿAlī al-Riḍā عليه السلام, whose Ziyāra is possible for them.

18. Love and Devotion Towards Ahl al-Bayt

May this love and devotion towards Ahl al-Bayt عليهم السلام remain in our hearts, and may we leave this world with their love still in our hearts.

19. At the Foot of the Pulpit of the Infallibles

Why do us Shīʿas not sit at the foot of the pulpit of the Commander of the Faithful, the Imāms of Guidance, and the Messenger of God عليهم السلام, every day, and listen to their words of wisdom, ethics, and the unlimited knowledge that is hidden in their words.

20. Visiting One is like Visiting All

If one visits one of the shrines of Ahl al-Bayt عليهم السلام, it is as though he has visited all the shrines in all the places and this is beneficial for him.

21. Seeking Intercession with the Imāmzadahs

Tawassul [seeking an intermediary] is very beneficial. Visit these Imāmzadahs [the descendants of the Imāms]! Just like fruits, each of which has an important vitamin, these great men too have specific characteristics and effects.

22. Everything from Love

One must not let go of his love for Ahl al-Bayt عليهم السلام. Everything is in their love; if we have anything, it is because of their love.

23. Our Responsibility During the Days of ʿĪd

On the night of ʿĪd al-Ghadīr and other similar nights, rather than spending sessions in laughter, play, and diversion, the virtues of these days and nights and the vices of their enemies, as well as the narrations regarding Wilāya should be mentioned with logical reasoning so that it would strengthen the religious beliefs of the listeners.

24. Do Not Be Deprived

One of the virtues of Shīʿa is the graves of the Imāmzadahs (the descendants of the Imāms); therefore, we must not be heedless of them and end up intentionally depriving ourselves.

25. Manifestations of the Extensive Mercy of God

God عزّ وجلّ knows [best] how extensive the mercy of Ahl al-Bayt and the progeny of the Prophet is عليهم السلام! Their Mercy is in line with the Extensive Mercy of God عزّ وجلّ.

26. Most Important Ethic of Ziyāra

The most important ethic of Ziyāra is for us to know that there is no difference between the life of the Imāms عليهم السلام and their death.

27. Present Everywhere

If one seeks to quench his thirst of meeting the Infallibles عليهم السلام then visiting the shrines of Ahl al-Bayt عليهم السلام is like meeting them, and Imām Muḥammad al-Mahdī عجّل الله تعالى فرجه الشريف. They are present and watching [us] everywhere.

28. Hearing the Response of Salām

It has been heard and seen that some individuals said Salām to the Infallible عليهم السلام whose shrine they were visiting, and heard a reply in return.

29. Most Valuable *Mustaḥab*

Weeping on the afflictions of Ahl al-Bayt عليهم السلام, and especially Imām al-Ḥusayn عليه السلام may be of the Mustaḥabbat better than which there is no other

Mustaḥab. 'Crying out of fear of God' is the same; it might not be superior to it.

30. True Love

True love is that there is no opposing love in it. Anyone that has love towards any of the fourteen Infallibles ☽ his work is done [he's felicitous]. The only condition is that his love should be true.

31. Distance from the Words of the Infallibles

The more we get away from the words of the Infallibles ☽, the more we are far from themselves.

32. Knowledge, Ethics, Actions

The Qur'ān should be in one of your hands, and Ahl al-Bayt ☽ [i.e. their teachings] in the other!

The teachings of Ahl al-Bayt ☽ are in the likes of *Nahj al-Balāgha* (The Peak of Eloquence). Their actions are written in the likes of *Al-Ṣaḥīfa al-Sajjādīyya*. Their obligatory rituals are in the likes of *Risālah al-ʿAmaliyyah Amaliyyah* (Book of Islamic Laws).

33. The Reward of Visiting Imām al-Ḥusayn

Do we know what the reward for visiting Imām al-Ḥusayn عليه السلام is? Do we know where the narrations mentioned for visiting Imām al-Ḥusayn عليه السلام have reached? Do we know what it means that "visiting Imām al-Ḥusayn on a Thursday night is like visiting God on His Throne?" Do we understand these things? [Do we understand] how much reward there is in crying for Imām al-Ḥusayn عليه السلام? Can we claim a limit for it beyond which there would not be anything else?

Concerning the Love for Imām Muḥammad al-Mahdī عجل الله تعالى فرجه الشريف

34. Perfect Manifestation of God

The Imām of the Time عجل الله تعالى فرجه الشريف is "God's witnessing eye, hearing-ear, expressive-tongue and open-hand."

35. Reason Behind the Occultation of the Imām

We ourselves are the reason behind the occultation of the Imām عجل الله تعالى فرجه الشريف.

36. The Steadfast Before the Reappearance of the Imām

There will be special blessings and favors for those that remain steadfast in their faith and religion before the reappearance of the Imām عجل الله تعالى فرجه الشريف.

37. Better than Meeting

It is not necessary for one to be striving to see Imām al-Mahdi عجل الله تعالى فرجه الشريف; rather, offering two rakʿat of prayers and then doing tawassul (seeking intersession) to the Holy Infallibles عليهم السلام may perhaps be better than meeting the Imām عجل الله تعالى فرجه الشريف.

38. We Must Seek Refuge in Him

We are on the verge of drowning in the sea of life, and we are in need of the assistance of God's Wali (authority) عجل الله تعالى فرجه الشريف in order to reach the destination safely. We must seek help from Imām al-Mahdi عجل الله تعالى فرجه الشريف so that he may lighten the path for us, and take us with himself, to the destination.

39. Remedy to All Pains

Praying for the faraj [i.e. praying for the hastening of relief and the reappearance of the Imām] is the remedy to all our pains.

40. The Doors of Meeting the Imām are Not Closed

During the period of occultation too the blessings and favors of the Imām عجل الله تعالى فرجه الشريف have been seen towards his lovers and followers. The doors of meeting him are not completely shut; in fact, even witnessing him physically cannot be denied.

41. What Answer do We Have?

Can we escape divine witnessing or hide ourselves, or carry out every act that we feel like, despite believing in a Master عجل الله تعالى فرجه الشريف that is 'God's witnessing eye'? How will we answer them?

42. We are Aware of Our Conduct

Even though Imām al-Mahdi عجل الله تعالى فرجه الشريف is hidden from us, and we are deprived of the blessings of his presence, we are aware of the acts that are or are not in accordance with his school and ways. We also know whether we please him with our acts and conduct and, although meager, send salutations to him, or displease him with our unworthy acts.

43. It is Not Unlikely

They have mentioned certain and uncertain signs of the reappearance of the Imām عجل الله تعالى فرجه الشريف; but it is not unlikely for them to inform us that he عجل الله تعالى فرجه الشريف shall re-appear tomorrow. The consequence of this is that alteration of the Divine Will would take place in some of the signs, whilst some of the imminent signs would occur right at the time of reappearance.

44. More Compassionate than Parents

How benevolent is the Imām ﷺ to those who utter his name, call upon him, and seek his help; he is more compassionate to them than their own parents are.

45. The Blessed Du'ā'

'Aẓumal-Bala' wa Bariḥal-Khafa'

عظم البلاء وبرح الخفاء

Recite specifically this blessed Du'ā' and ask God ﷻ to bring us the Possessor of Affairs.[11]

46. The Sweetness of Reappearance

May God ﷻ sweeten the mouth of all the Shī'as with the reappearance of the hidden Imām ﷺ! Sweets are foods that are beyond our necessities, but the sweetness of the reappearance of Imām al-Mahdi ﷺ is of the greatest of necessities.

[11] Full Du'ā' added at the end of the book.

47. We Must Pray

Should we not ponder and pray with grief and humility for the arrival of the true reformer, and relief for the Muslims, i.e. Imām al-Mahdi عجل الله تعالى فرجه الشريف?

48. The Most Important Du'ā'

More important than praying for the hastening of the reappearance of Imām al-Mahdi عجل الله تعالى فرجه الشريف is to pray for our faith, steadfastness in our beliefs, and not denying the Imām عجل الله تعالى فرجه الشريف until his reappearance.

49. Imām's Request for Prayers

It is a pity that everyone goes to Masjid Jamkarān for the fulfillment of his or her personal desires, whilst he or she does not know how the Imām عجل الله تعالى فرجه الشريف himself requests them to pray for the hastening of his reappearance.

50. Necessity of Having a Relationship with the Imām

Everyone should be worried about his own self and find a way for establishing a relationship with the Imām عجل الله تعالى فرجه الشريف and for his own aid, regardless of whether Imām's عجل الله تعالى فرجه الشريف reappearance is near or far.

51. The Real Green Island

Wherever the Imām ﷺ is, it is green. The heart of a believer is the Green Island. Wherever he (a believer) is, the Imām ﷺ treads there.

52. A Cultivated Heart is the Place of the Imām's Presence

Hearts are dried because of the lack of faith, and the light of cognizance. Cultivate hearts with faith and the remembrance of God ﷻ, so that the presence of Imām al-Mahdi ﷺ in the heart be approved for you.

53. Those Who are Truly Awaiting

They want people that are only for Imām al-Mahdi ﷺ. Only those who are waiting for the sake of God ﷻ, and in the way of God ﷻ, and not for the fulfillment of their personal desires, are those who are really waiting for the reappearance.

54. The Result of Acting Upon that which is Certain

If we act according to that which is certain in religion, at the time of sleeping and self-accounting we will identify which of our deeds definitely please the Imām ﷺ, and which of them definitely displease him ﷺ.

55. Do We Seek Awareness and Meeting the Imām?

Indeed, those that are thirsty receive the drop of reunion, and the seekers of beauty are given the drink of eternal life and cognizance. Are we thirsty for cognizance and seek to meet him عجل الله تعالى فرجه الشريف and he عجل الله تعالى فرجه الشريف does not give us from the spring of life despite the fact that he عجل الله تعالى فرجه الشريف is responsible for being just to all and looks after the pain-stricken people of the entire world?

56. Self-Building—the Path to Joining

The Holy Infallibles عليهم السلام have said, "Reform yourselves, and we ourselves will come to you; you do not need to be looking for us."

57. The Path of Salvation

Our affairs will not be solved until we do not have a strong relationship with the Imām of our time عجل الله تعالى فرجه الشريف. The strength of our relationship with the Imām عجل الله تعالى فرجه الشريف is also in reforming ourselves.

58. Those Who Supplicate for the Relief

It is narrated that during the period of occultation everyone shall perish except those that pray for the relief. It is as though this very supplication for the relief is a source of hope and spiritual relationship with him who is prayed for. This in itself is a level of relief.

59. The Imām's Mosque

How much should we say that Imām al-Mahdi عجل الله تعالى فرجه الشريف has a Mosque in the heart of every Shīʿa.

60. Everyone is Concerned about Himself

All of us are concerned about their own personal desires, and we are not concerned about the Imām عجل الله تعالى فرجه الشريف, whilst being concerned for him is beneficial for all, and is of the greatest of necessities.

61. Because of Our Deeds

It is because of our sins and deeds that the Imām عجل الله تعالى فرجه الشريف is fearful and wandering in deserts for a thousand years.

62. Asking for the Most Important Need

Whoever goes to a sacred place, such as Masjid Jamkarān, for a need, must first ask God عزّ وجلّ for the Imām's عجل الله تعالى فرجه الشريف relief, which is the greatest desire of the Imām himself.

63. To which Group do We Belong?

In the records of Imām al-Mahdi عجل الله تعالى فرجه الشريف, who is presented with the deeds of the people twice a week (on Mondays and Thursdays), God عزّ وجلّ knows best which group we belong to. All we do know is that we are not that which we should be.

64. A Group of People Always has Relations with Him

The sun is meant to shine even though it may be behind the clouds. Imām al-Mahdi عجل الله تعالى فرجه الشريف is the same, even though he may be in occultation! We do not see him عجل الله تعالى فرجه الشريف but there were, and still are people that see him عجل الله تعالى فرجه الشريف, and if they do not see him عجل الله تعالى فرجه الشريف, they have some form of contact with him عجل الله تعالى فرجه الشريف.

65. He Cries while We Laugh

Is it possible for our Master, Imām al-Mahdi عجل الله تعالى فرجه الشريف to be grieved, and for us to be happy; for him to weep because of the afflictions of his friends, and for us to laugh and be cheerful; and despite all of this, consider ourselves his followers?

66. The Whispers of the Lovers

I wish we would sit and talk about the time of the reappearance of Imām al-Mahdi عجل الله تعالى فرجه الشريف so that we would at least be regarded as those awaiting his عجل الله تعالى فرجه الشريف reappearance.

67. The True Refuge

If the believers recognize their true place of refuge and seek refuge in it, is it still possible that they will not be blessed by it?

68. Referring to the Imām in all Affairs

Despite the fact that we do not receive revelations and inspiration, we do not pay attention to that intermediary of Divine Blessings who does receive revelations and inspirations; and this is despite the fact that we can resort to him عجّل الله تعالى فرجه الشريف for all our difficulties, regardless of whether spiritual or physical, worldly, or of the hereafter.

69. Pray for Me

Imām al-Mahdi عجّل الله تعالى فرجه الشريف has the highest degree of knowledge, and the greatest Divine Name (Al-I'sm Al-Aʿẓam) is with him more than everyone else; yet, he has asked everyone that has been blessed with his visitation, whilst awake or in a dream, "Pray for me!"

70. The Sole Way of Getting Rid of Difficulties

The sole way of getting rid of difficulties is to pray for the reappearance of Imām al-Mahdi عجّل الله تعالى فرجه الشريف in solitude, not the usual prayers and the movement of the tongue; rather prayers with sincerity and purity of intention, accompanied with repentance.

71. Meeting the Imām

Question: I am eager to meet the Imām of our time, Imām al-Mahdi عجل الله تعالى فرجه الشريف. I request you to pray for the fulfillment of this desire of mine.

Answer: Recite ṣalawāt a lot and present them to him عجل الله تعالى فرجه الشريف, along with praying for the hastening of his عجل الله تعالى فرجه الشريف reappearance. In addition, go to Masjid Jamkarān a lot, and offer the prayers of the Masjid.

The Secrets of Prayers and Supplications

72. The Best Time of Meeting

Prayers are the best time for meeting and being in the presence of God عزّ وجلّ. Prayers have been established for submission and humility with all its stages.

73. The Greatest Manifestations of Servitude

Prayers are the greatest manifestation of servitude in which there's great attention to God عزّ وجلّ.

74. Every Prayer Better than the Previous Prayer

Perhaps the wisdom behind repeating prayers, other than consolidation, is wayfaring such that every prayer is better than the previous one and the previous prayer paves the way for the next prayer.

75. Sajdah, the Point of Extreme Humility

The standing of a servant during prayers is the sign of servitude and tranquility, and that he has no movement from his own self, and Sajdah is the epitome of humility.

76. Acquiring the Presence of Heart

Q: Please tell us how the presence of the heart is acquired.

A: In the Name of the Most High ﷻ. If what is meant is the presence of heart, then it is acquired by offering supererogatory prayers, and recommended acts, as well as offering prayers in congregation. The presence of heart is acquired by not pressurizing oneself during heedlessness, and when it is acquired, one must not lose it optionally.

77. Presence of Heart and Concentration

Q: Please give us instructions for acquiring the presence of heart and concentration in prayers.

A: In the Name of the Most High عزّ وجلّ.The moment you realize, do not give up optionally.

78. Seeking the Intercession of the Imām Before Prayers

Reforming the prayers means reforming its apparent as well as its inner reality, and refraining from apparent and hidden evils. Amongst the ways of reforming prayers is seeking the intercession of the Imām عجّل الله تعالى فرجه الشريف seriously, just before starting the prayers.

79. Reciters of Night Prayers

It is as though those who perform night prayers have overtaken secretly.

80. Success in Performing Night Prayers

Q: What should we do to be successful at offering night prayers?

A: If it is not achieved by taking efforts at reciting the last verse of Sūrat al-Kahf, then it should be offered in the first half of the night (i.e. before midnight).

﴿قُل إِنَّمَا أَنَا بَشَرٌ مِثلُكُم يوحىٰ إِلَيَّ أَنَّمَا إِلٰهُكُم إِلٰهٌ واحِدٌ فَمَن كانَ يَرجو لِقاءَ رَبِّهِ فَليَعمَل عَمَلًا صالِحًا وَلا يُشرِك بِعِبادَةِ رَبِّهِ أَحَدًا﴾

﴿qul ʾinnamā ʾana basharun mithlukum yūḥā ʾilayya ʾannamā ʾilāhukum ʾilāhun wāḥidun fa-man kāna yarjū liqāʾa rabbihī fa-l-yaʿmal ʿamalan ṣāliḥan wa-lā yushrik bi-ʿibādati rabbihī ʾaḥadan﴾

﴿Say, *'I am just a human being like you. It has been revealed to me that your God is the One God. So whoever expects to encounter his Lord —let him act righteously, and not associate anyone with the worship of his Lord.'*﴾[12]

81. Way of Getting Rid of Laziness

Q: I am slightly lazy in performing night prayers and rising before dawn, please guide me!

A: In the Name of the Most High ﷻ. Laziness of offering night prayers will be solved by deciding to perform its Qaḍāʾ prayers every time you fail to offer it [at its time].

82. The True Prayers

From the verse 'Indeed the prayer restrains from indecent and wrongful conduct,' it is learnt that 'one

---

[12] Sūrat al-Kahf, Verse 110.

who does not refrain from unworthy acts, his prayers are not the true prayers.'

83. The Pleasure in Prayers

There are a series of preliminaries, both inside and outside prayers, which would help one feel the pleasure in prayers. That which needs to be paid attention before and outside prayers is that one must refrain from committing sins, and not blacken his heart. Sins sadden the soul and take away the light from the heart. As for during the prayers, one must set up chains around himself so that no one besides God ﷻ enters the heart; in other words, he must not think about anyone other than God ﷻ.

84. Presence of Heart During Prayers

One of the factors for acquiring the presence of heart during prayers is to keep all our senses under control during the twenty-four hours, in order to provide the basis for the acquisition of the presence of heart. Throughout the day, we must keep our eyes, ears, and all our other parts under control.

85. Prayer Is Sweeter than Everything

The same prayers that we perform with the threat of being caned and whipped, and with the fear of being punished in hell (as a result of missing them), some say, "It is sweeter than everything."

86. Ascend with Prayers

These apparent and easy deeds such as prayers help some ascend to the Heavens; and for some it is nothing! For some, it is the A'la 'Illiyīn (the highest of the Heavens), whilst others cannot understand if this confection is salty or sweet!

87. Carrying Out Our Responsibilities in the Best Way

Q: I would like to understand and perceive all the dhikr (invocations) and witness the light and perceive it, in order to be able to walk with that light!

A: In the Name of the Most High ﷻ. Carry out your deeds with all the conditions for the presence of heart, what they will give you in reward has nothing to do with us!

88. We are Nothing

Sajdah is the epitome of humility – [it implies] that we are nothing before you.

89. Entering the Divine Sanctuary

Dhikr (invocation of God) in prayers is the best dhikr, since prayers are at the position of the Kaʿbah; one who prays has entered the divine sanctuary of God and has intended to enter from the gate of Takbīr (Allahu Akbar) and exit from the gate of Taslīm (the last Salām of prayers).

Concerning Ethics and Spiritual Wayfaring

90. Intimacy with the Qur'ān and Ahl al-Bayt

May we have an inward warmth and intimacy with the Noble Qur'ān, religion, and the necessities and preliminaries of religiosity, and may the Qur'ān and Ahl al-Bayt be sufficient for us so that we become certain of the rightfulness of religion.

91. Effect of the Verses of Blessings and Punishments

Some of those who were brought close to God have died out of the love of visiting paradise, because listening to the verses of blessing and bounties or punishment and vengeance surely leaves an ontological effect in a Monotheist.

92. The States of the People of Spirituality

God knows best the state of those who have spiritual stations at the time of supplication and solitude; and how the silence of pondering burns them as a result of witnessing the divine lights, even if for a short duration.

93. With the All-Needless

In obeying the commands of God ﷻ and in committing sins and obeying the commands of Satan and the self, is it better to be in the company of he in whose hands is our life and death, wealth and poverty, sickness and wellbeing, doctor, treasures, wealth, etc. [...] or he who has nothing?!

94. True Meaning of Obedience and Sinfulness

For the ease of obedience and avoidance of sins, we have no other way than to know and be certain of the fact that obedience is the nearness to all bounties, pleasures, wealth, and honor whilst sinfulness is privation, displeasure, destitution and dishonor [...]

95. Lack of Contradiction

Grief, supplication, and tawassul (seeking intercession) have no contradiction with surrendering and submission to the Divine Decree.

96. Seeker of Maʿrifah (*Divine Cognizance*)

If one deserves it, meaning that he is eager to seek *Maʿrifah* (Divine Cognizance), and if he has endeavor and a sincerity of intention, with the permission of God ﷻ, all of creation would become his teacher.

97. Teachings of the Imāms

Our Imāms عليهم السلام have taught us to act upon certainties and to halt and take precaution in whatever we are not sure about.

98. Benefitting from Every Noble Act

It is good that man has his name written in every noble act and takes part in it, for he does not know which one will be accepted and which one rejected on the Day of Judgment!

99. Reflecting on the Quality of Good Acts

Man must think about ways of carrying out good acts, and this should bring about initiatives helpful for reaching the goal.

100. Man's Heedlessness of Death

How close man is to death, yet how far does he see it from himself and is heedless of it!

101. Journeying Through Purgatory

Every night, we journey through purgatory without having any authority, yet we are heedless of death!

102. Good State at the Time of Death

Felicitous are those who die in a good state, and are welcomed nicely in the hereafter!

103. Dominance of the Disbelievers over Muslims

Resemblance and integration with disbelievers makes their dominance and authority over Muslims easier.

104. A Loving Cycle of the Qur'ān and Ahl al-Bayt

May there arise within us love for the entire Qur'ān, and Ahl al-Bayt عليهم السلام, so that primarily, we are able to find the oneness of the Qur'ān and Ahl al-Bayt عليهم السلام and the confected composite of the two; and secondly, at the level of following and acting upon them, we perform a loving cycle on their basis and whilst paying attention to them, and that we come to realize that they are the worthiest of being loved compared to every other beloved.

105. Capability of Acquiring Perfection

Man is capable of acquiring all the stations of the Prophets ﻋﻠﻴﻬﻢ ﺍﻟﺴﻼﻡ except the specific stations of the special Prophets ﻋﻠﻴﻬﻢ ﺍﻟﺴﻼﻡ.

106. Main Reason Behind Man's Imperfection

Man's imperfection is due to his obeying the self and his distance from the teachings and obedience of the Prophets ﻋﻠﻴﻬﻢ ﺍﻟﺴﻼﻡ.

107. Effect of Contentment

It is impossible for one who does not take to contentment to be satisfied with that which he has! On the other hand, if one is content, his needs shall be fulfilled, even if they are a lot!

108. Feeling the Need of Praying

Is it possible that we feel the need for praying for the difficulties of the believers in the same manner, or even more than we feel the need for bread and water at the time of hunger and thirst?

109. Tending to the Affairs of Muslims

Can we be felicitous while being indifferent to the affairs of Muslims and believers?! Is it possible to reach the goal without tending to the affairs of Muslims?

110. Importance of Taking Precaution

There is no act in which taking precaution would bring about regret.

111. Paying Attention to Bounties and Afflictions

The poor should have patience in poverty and destitution, and they should know that they have other bounties that the rich do not have, and that the rich have difficulties and afflictions that the poor and the destitute do not have.

112. Inner Ease and Peacefulness of the Heart

The goodness of pleasure is not only due to the excess of ease; inward ease, welfare, and peacefulness of the heart are not acquired by having ease and luxury; rather, ease and luxury too may bring about anxiety and distress!

113. Materials—A Means to Spirituality

May it be such that worldly materials are only a means for us, in a way that if the world welcomes us, it causes us to pay more attention to spirituality and the Hereafter.

114. The Future of Our Children

Some scholars would secure the future of their children by recommending the offering of prayers at their time and night prayers.

115. The Means of Acquiring Peacefulness of the Heart

Having means of ease and luxury is other than having peacefulness of the heart, "Indeed hearts find rest in God's remembrance!"

﴿أَلَا بِذِكْرِ اللَّهِ تَطْمَئِنُّ الْقُلُوبُ﴾

﴿a-lā bi-dhikri llāhi taṭma'innu l-qulūb[u]﴾

﴿The hearts find rest in God's remembrance!﴾[13]

This means that the only means of peacefulness of the heart is dhikrollah (Remembrance of God); but we rely on other causes and are neglectful of the Cause of all causes.

116. If We Do Not Supplicate

If we remain indifferent and do not pray for the relief of believers from the troubles and afflictions

---

[13] Sūrat al-Ra'd, Verse 28.

encountered by them, those afflictions will get closer to us also.

117. These Simple and Brief Acts of Worship

God ﷻ knows best the effect that these short and brief acts of worship have, if carried out by those worthy of it.

118. Biographies of the Scholars of the Past

Referring to the biographies of the scholars of the past is like referring to authentic books on ethics.

119. May We Realize that We are Spoiled

May God ﷻ grant us the Tawfīq (Divine Assistance) that if we are caught in the midst of afflictions and tests, we do not see the bad as good and the good as bad. We are spoiled; may it be such that we realize that we are spoiled, so that we begin thinking about reforming and curing ourselves.

120. The Perfection of Man

The perfection of man lies in piety, not a word less or more than that.

121. God's Mercy

How much of God's ﷻ mercy is for those who are not indifferent and pray and cry for the relief of Muslims and believers from the afflictions that befall them.

122. Loftier than Angels

If one observes his duties, he is loftier than angels, and no longer must he be worried.

123. Value of Supplication

Our Infallibles عليهم السلام have left supplications at our disposal in order to see us dwelling in light.

124. Method of the Prophets

The prophets, peace be upon them, have come in order to distance us as well as our attention from the world.

125. We must seek Refuge in God

That was Satan's end after six thousand years of worship; can we then be proud of ourselves?! We seek refuge in God ﷻ!

126. Our Remedy

If only we understood that our remedy lies in one thing only, and that is to identify the divine obligations and know which acts to carry out, and which ones to refrain from.

127. The Obstacles to the Acceptance of Deeds

Pride, arrogance, and jealousy are obstacles to acceptance of our deeds, because God ﷻ says,

﴿إِنَّمَا يَتَقَبَّلُ اللَّهُ مِنَ الْمُتَّقِينَ﴾

﴾'innamā yataqabbalu llāhu mina l-muttaqīn[a]﴿

﴾God accepts only from the Godwary﴿[14]

128. We must not be Discouraged in the Path of Truth

Unworthy abuses and insults should not upset, discourage, and leave us lazy from the path and goal.

129. Always with Him

God ﷻ wants us to be with Him ﷻ at all times and remain connected to the spring; and this is to our benefit.

---

[14] Sūrat al-Mā'idah, Verse 27.

130. Our Responsibility

Our responsibility is only to carry out al-amr bi al-maʿrūf [i.e. enjoin the good] and wa al-nahy ʿan al-munkar [forbid the evil] where possible; but its results are not in our hands.

131. The Effect of Some Afflictions

What do we know! God ﷻ knows that some afflictions are the prerequisite of some blessings. Someone would say, "I got afflicted with such and such difficulty and it increased my knowledge."

132. Greater than the Night Prayers

In my [humble] opinion, crying for the sake of Imām al-Ḥusayn ؑ is higher in virtue than the night prayers.

133. Crying and Grief

Grief, sorrow, and crying are acts of the heart, so much so that crying and tears are signs of the acceptance of the Witr prayers.[15]

[15] The last rakʿah of the Night prayers.

134. The Best State and Deeds

We must resort to every such act that improves our state and increases our attention towards God ﷿, and we must occupy ourselves with those acts, the remembrance of God ﷿, self-scrutiny and paying attention to God ﷿.

135. Sincere Preachers

Those who, like the prophets, have been appointed to preaching, and carry out their work without any favors and obligations, God ﷿ knows best what ranks they hold! Of course, this is only if the scholar is aware of the do's and don'ts and he himself practices that which he encourages and forbids.

136. Value the Opportunity

When one is given the chance to teach, study, or write, he must value the opportunity.

137. Light of the Intellect

The principles and acts of religion can be proven through the light of the intellect. Those who oppose intellectual principles and proofs in fact promote irreligionism, because 'there is no religion for he who has no intellect.'

138. The Season Behind Salmān's Greatness

Salmān ﷺ knew the first and the last knowledge as a result of learning the obligations, abiding by them, and obeying the religion with the light of intellect.

139. After the Trial

The religiosity of a person comes to be known when he finds himself choosing between the world or the hereafter, and obeying Satan and the self or serving God ﷻ.

140. An Important Warning

Woe upon us if we use spirituality as a means to reach our material and transient desires!

141. Protecting our Faith

How bound must the pious be in order to refrain from acting upon that which is uncertain! Protecting one's faith is like walking on fire or holding fire in one's hands.

142. Creating Warmth and Serenity at Home

If we want the environment in the house to be warm, pure, and friendly, we have to be patient, steadfast, forbearing, forgiving, and benevolent, so that warmth and blessings prevail in the house.

143. Occupying Ourselves with Our Own Faults

Fortunate is he who sees his own faults, and pays attention to his own vices, ignores other's faults, and does not see himself as perfect and without defects.

144. Do Not Justify

We must close the door of justifying our wrongdoings and repent for every sin, and compensate for it wherever possible.

145. A Dangerous Illness

May it not happen that ḥarām becomes attractive to man! This is a disease of the soul that man is afflicted with such that he is caught up in ḥarām despite there being numerous ḥalāl ways for fulfilling his needs.

146. Through His Own Will

Man, through his own will, can become either the companion of Salmān or that of Abu Jahl.

147. The Path of Salvation

The path of salvation is to escape and return to God ﷻ and His Authorities.

148. O Soul at Peace

If man's heart acquires peace with the remembrance of God ﷻ, it will be addressed thus:

﴿يا أَيَّتُهَا النَّفسُ الْمُطمَئِنَّةُ﴾

﴿yā-'ayyatuhā n-nafsu l-muṭma'innat^u﴾

﴿'O soul at peace!﴾[16]

149. Harm of Knowledge Not Connected to Revelation

Without revelation and the teachings of the Prophets ﵈ man's knowledge has greater harm than benefits.

150. In Afflictions

When encountered by afflictions, we must look into the book of Sharī'a at each and every step. Wherever there is clarity, we should step forward and act upon it, and in places of doubt, we must halt.

[16] Sūrat al-Fajr, Verse 27.

151. Do Not Leave Today's Work for Tomorrow

It is good for man to not postpone today's work for tomorrow, rather, to not delay the work of a certain time to another hour, unless with an excuse, for he does not know what would happen after that time.

152. Necessity of Avoiding *Ḥarām* Food

Woe upon us if we do not avoid eating and drinking ḥarām, for it is our food that becomes the cause of our knowledge and faith, or disbelief.

153. The Effect of Food on the Self

God ﷻ knows best how much involvement food has on one's belief and disbelief, and good and bad deeds.

154. Tribulations Due to Weeping

God Himself ﷻ sends tribulations,

﴿فَلَوْلاَ إِذْ جَاءَهُم بَأْسُنَا تَضَرَّعُوا﴾

﴾fa-law-lā 'idh jā'ahum ba'sunā taḍarra'ū﴿

﴾*Why did they not entreat when*
Our punishment overtook them!﴿[17]

out of entreaty, i.e. He ﷻ wants His servant to entreat and lament to him, and this is desired.

155. Progress Through Supplications

If you want to reach somewhere [i.e. higher stations] through supplications, then you must be saying this: "We surrender to God, let Him do whatever He intends to, we intend to act according to the responsibilities of servitude."

156. Effects of *Murāqaba* (Attentive Observation)

God ﷻ knows best the effects that murāqaba (attentive observation) and attention have on man's soul and in the acquisition of knowledge and maʿrifa (Divine Knowledge).

157. Best State (of Spirituality) and Cognizance

There is no doubt in the fact that if one pays attention to this one point it would suffice for him and it entails all the meanings and results of exercising strict self-control. The point is that man sees himself in the presence of God ﷻ and acknowledges that God ﷻ is

[17] Sūrat al-Anʿām, Verse 43.

aware of him, present everywhere and an observer of all of his states and deeds."

158. The Prolongation of the Path Due to Our Sins

All of us have a distance to the ultimate goal and destination. We must try not to make the distance longer or our load heavier. Sins make the load heavier and our distance to the destination longer!

159. Afflictions—the Result of Ingratitude of Bounties

All these plights and afflictions are the result of thanklessness and ingratitude for our bounties.

160. Gratitude for Bounties bring about Increase

Gratitude causes an increase in bounties, and if you do not thank (God), there will be no increase (in bounties). Therefore, if we do not see any increase (in bounties), we should know that it is because of the lack of thankfulness.

161. The Meaning of Gratitude and Ingratitude

Gratitude for bounties means obedience to God ﷻ, which leads to an increase in bounties. Ingratitude means disobedience to God ﷻ and this leads to divine punishment.

162. Cutting off from All, and Joining the Friend

If one cuts off his attention and relation with all other than God ﷻ, his relation with God ﷻ would be definite.

163. Relationship with Scholars and Recognition of God

If our distance from [religious] scholars increases, we will no longer be curable. Scholar implies one who recognizes God ﷻ and is an active, religious scholar, not just one who wears a turban.

164. The Effect of Good Behavior

By observing true Islamic ethics and behavior, even non-Muslims will be attracted to Islam and Muslims.

165. The Advantage of Humility and *Tawassul*

During the times of ease, we must have the state of humility, lamentation, tawassul (seeking intersession) and be thankful, so that they help us during times of intensity and affliction, else we will encounter those plights and afflictions.

166. Deprivation from Divine Blessings

Not carrying out good acts such as giving alms and building charity organizations, mosques, Ḥusayniyas, baths, schools and hospitals and ..., which people are deprived of nowadays, is not due to lack of money; rather, it is out of the lack of divine blessings.

167. All of It is Mercy

The afflictions that befall us are all mercy; in the least, they are the causes of the atonement of our sins.

168. A Great Supplication

This is a great supplication and we have been ordered to recite it during the period of occultation: "Yā Allāh, Yā Rahmān, Yā Rahīm, Yā Muqallib al-Qulūb, Thabbit Qalbī 'alā dīnik." (O God, O Beneficent, O Merciful, O turner of Hearts, make my heart steadfast in your religion!)

169. God's Grace, Always and for All

Ilhām (*Divine Inspiration*) is a great stage at the level of revelation; we are not seekers (of divine blessings), else divine blessings are never cut off.

170. Not Grieving for Other than God

It is very good if God ﷻ grants man such a strength and will that he does not grieve for other than God ﷻ. This requires courage, faith, and steadfastness.

171. From the Effects of Honesty

Honesty is very effective in seeing true dreams and in spiritual purity.

172. Relationship with God and His Close Servants

Is it possible for one to have religious and spiritual relationship with God ﷻ and His close servants, and not be helped in critical times, rather, left disheartened and without guidance?

173. Solution During Difficulties

In times of difficulties and afflictions, man has no option but to seek the intercession of God ﷻ, and take refuge in Him ﷻ every moment.

174. Attachment to Superstitions

Look at what the worshippers of this world have attached themselves to and fight over; a world of paper, carton, and cobwebs!

175. The True Meaning of *Zuhd* (Abstinence)

Practicing zuhd is not in conflict with having the world; the criterion in zuhd is not having or not having the world; rather, it is attaching or not attaching oneself to the world.

176. The Path of Perfection is Open

The door to reaching perfection and meeting God ﷻ is open. Is it not a pity to not have and be deprived of these stages, which are gained through the servitude of God ﷻ?

177. The Need for Steadfastness in the Path of Truth

The minority of the people of truth, and the majority of the people of falsehood, must not worry, discourage, or prevent us from traversing the path of truth.

178. One Must Not Become Proud

We must not become proud! Until the time of death, and as long as Satan is alive, man is in danger. We seek refuge in God ﷻ.

179. A Moment of Separation

If man is left to himself for the blink of an eye, he would be separated from God ﷻ, and Satan will do his job and deceive him.

180. Departure is Close

Bidding farewell to this world is very close for us; however, we see it as very far, else we would not have so many conflicts with each other.

181. Man's Enmity with Himself

Man does with himself that with no enemy does with him; he dries the source of self-reform until the Day of Judgment!

182. Blessings and Strengthening of the Faith

God ﷻ strengthens the faith of those who remain steadfast in times of difficulties, so they are not defeated by any affliction, and they leave this world with faith, remembrance, and the love of God ﷻ.

183. Trust in God

Man cannot achieve peace through anything other than trust in God ﷻ and His ﷻ remembrance; and nothing makes life bitter and horrible the way heedlessness and turning away from His v remembrance does.

184. Importance of Recognizing One's Responsibilities

Have we found the path of God ﷻ and servitude so that we stay on the path?!

Recognition of responsibilities is a light in the heart of a believer. If he acts upon his obligations, imprisonment and torture would be easy for him.

185. Vanity of this Contingent World

If only we understood the vanity of this contingent world and that we would not give so much value and importance to 'nothing', and that we would not have so many disputes with each other over 'nothing'!

186. The Effect of Doubtful Food

Eating doubtful food, as well as eating the food of one, who does not abstain from *ḥarām*, although permissible, makes a man ill and prevents him from worship, or causes him to become the cause of the loss of tawfīq (Divine Assistance).

187. We Alter the Mercy

If we do not become bad, that which descends upon us from above will not become bad; rather we do things that change the rains of mercy into punishment.

188. Our Benevolent and Spiritual Fathers

We must be loyal to the Shīʿa scholars. They are our benevolent and spiritual kind fathers and they have many rights upon us.

189. The Acquisition of Praiseworthy Attributes

We must strive to acquire patience, forbearance, and humility, and refrain from having others respect us out of fear.

190. Meeting God with the Eyes of Insight

If meeting God ﷻ is possible in the Hereafter, then so it is even in this world, with the same criterion of possibility; however not with the physical eyes, rather with the eyes of the heart and insight.

191. The Possibility of Acquiring Proximity

Man can traverse the straight path of servitude in all circumstances and afflictions, and consequently, acquire proximity.

192. We Ourselves are the Cause of Heedlessness

We ourselves prepare the causes of danger, heedlessness, and forgetfulness of the remembrance of God ﷻ. The defects of our acts become apparent as a result of murāqaba (attentive observation) and muḥāsaba (reckoning).

193. Ascent and Descent

Man is worse than Satan in his descent and better than angels in his ascent.

194. High Aspirations

Those who had a little spirituality did not go after miracles.

195. The Greatest Alchemy

Why would one who is blessed with spirituality and maʿrifah (cognizance of God) need alchemy?! What alchemy is greater than the cognizance of God ﷻ?

196. Love—the Basis of Servitude

The basis of servitude is love; God ﷻ says,

﴿يُحِبُّهُمْ وَيُحِبُّونَهُ﴾

﴿*yuḥibbuhum wa-yuḥibbūnahū*﴾

﴿*whom He loves and who love Him*﴾[18]

197. Descent and Decline

Any path that a man takes without adhering to the Qur'ān and Sunnah, will lead him to a continuous decline.

198. The People of the Truth or the People of Falsehood

Man must determine his position every day, as to whether he is from amongst the followers of the people of the truth or the people of falsehood..

199. Possibility of Reaching the Summit of Perfections

God ﷻ has created Man in such a way that he can step higher than the rank of angels through sincere servitude, and acquire the ranks of the prophets and close servants of God ﷻ.

200. The Greatest Perfection of Man

Dhikr is the greatest perfection for man.

---

[18] Sūrat al-Mā'idah, Verse 54.

201. God's Grace for All

Every person has a bowl full of afflictions, which is in accordance with his own existence and capacity. Everyone's bowl is filled with afflictions, but God ﷻ loves everyone.

202. The Manner of Acquiring this World and Prosperity

The Prophets and the Imāms (ʿa) have not come to ask people not to benefit from the world at all; rather they have come to show us the manner of acquiring this world along with prosperity and honor.

203. Acquiring a Beneficial Job

May it be such that we can recognize a job beneficial for ourselves and find stability in it, and remain steadfast in it, and not have a new thought and idea every day.

204. Learn Lessons and Value Them

We must take lessons from the past generations in that we too, like them, are close to death; and we should not be under the false impression that the four days of our remaining life would be four hundred thousand years!

205. Seeing the Effects of Deeds

Man should be watchful of his deeds so that he sees their good and bad results.

206. Opportunity of Reforming Our Defects

With respect to all our vices and reforming them, we do not have the time to attend to our own daily vices, let alone others'.

207. First, Reforming Ourselves

We must be thinking about ourselves and reform ourselves. If we fail to reform ourselves, we would not be able to reform others.

208. Servitude of God Only

We must know that there is only one issue, and that is the servitude of God ﷻ; the servitude of God ﷻ lies in obedience to Him ﷻ, and obedience to Him ﷻ is in the abandonment of sins in beliefs and practice.

209. Dangerous World of Heedlessness

The world of heedlessness is the world of preparing oneself for the satans of the man and jinn.

210. In Need of Complete Protection

We must ask God ﷻ to protect us every moment from all spiritual, inward, outward, worldly and afterlife harms and afflictions.

211. Way of Reforming Affairs

If you reform yourself and get rid of the obstacles between you and God ﷻ, the Prophets عليهم السلام and His ﷻ close servants, then God ﷻ will reform (the relationships) between you and the people.

212. Cure to All Affairs

We must know that our cure in all stages is self-reform, such that we will never be needless of it, and without it, the difficulties of our affairs will never be solved.

213. Prayers of Angels for Man

If one really prays for the believers, and does not pray for himself, angels will pray for him.

214. Increase in Wealth

Paying the Divine Rights (such as khums, zakāt and ṣadaqa) causes the wealth to grow and be purified. If one does so, his money will increase.

215. Acquiring Religious Knowledge

Every individual should spend a part of his day acquiring religious knowledge, even if it is just for an hour, for instance.

216. The Virtues of Thankfulness

If one looks at those who are lower than he is and thanks God ﷻ, this thankfulness itself will bring him abundance. This thankfulness itself holds weight, and causes the poor to become rich.

217. State of the Reliant

Some regard reliance (on God) as sustenance for themselves, and in fact, such individuals are rich. They have come to understand that if they rely on God ﷻ, their sustenance will reach them, and if it doesn't reach, they realize that it was not necessary.

218. Ease

Abundance of wealth and being financially settled is a prerequisite and it allows man to live at ease. However, one who relies upon God ﷻ, lives at ease without the prerequisite.

219. The Reform of Society

It can be said that the reform of society is dependent upon the reformation of the teachers and preachers.

220. Abiding by Only that which is Certain

May God ﷻ grant us Divine Assistance so that we do not leave that which is certain, and only abide by that which is certain in all circumstances, whilst traveling, and when at home, for this will never bring regret.

221. It Has No Benefit Without *Murāqaba*

On the path of acquiring cognizance, one must practice murāqaba (attentive observation), and there is no benefit until he does not reach the state of murāqaba!

222. Obligatory Portion of Religious Knowledge

A small portion of acquiring religious knowledge is obligatory upon all, such that if one finds the need, he could refer to the books of Islamic Laws, and understand the solution to his problem.

223. Combination of Knowledge and Action

If knowledge is accompanied with action, there will not be a lack... Just the fact that one has acted in accordance with his knowledge means that he is not in a state of waiting anymore; everything else is upon God ﷻ.

224. A Warning to the Wayfarers

Do not be infatuated with stages of mysticism and miracles; sometimes such things will lead you to hell!

225. Danger of Lying and Backbiting

If the door to lying and backbiting is opened, sinning and transgression will have no limits.

226. Fear of Downfall

Those who have been brought close (to God) fear their downfall, and not only hellfire, "Suppose that I am able to endure Your chastisement, how will I endure separation from You?"[19]

[19] A phrase from Du'ā' Kumayl.

227. Annoying Satan

Lengthening one's prostration annoys Satan.

228. Benefits of Ṣadaqa

Afflictions are repelled by ṣadaqa, even though they may be strongly in place. This decrease (in wealth) is a cause for increase; it increases sustenance.

229. Purpose of Afflictions

Afflictions are for us to reach certainty.

230. Main Reason Behind Deviations

One who knows that he's being seen and heard by God ﷻ, cannot sin. All our deviations are because we do not see God ﷻ as a witness and an observer.

231. Like a Butterfly

Why are we not like butterflies, flying in search of spiritual light?

232. Importance of Aḥādīth

We must deal with aḥādīth (in our everyday life) and study them, for remedy is within them.

233. The Book *'Jihad al-Nafs'*

Read one Ḥadīth from the book 'Jihād al-Nafs' of Wasā'il al-Shī'a every day, and ponder more on its apparent meanings! Then you will see in yourself that you have changed over a year!

234. Best Advice

I have said repeatedly and I say again that one who knows that, 'whoever remembers God, God will be his companion,' needs no admonishment.

235. Action—the Lightener of Our Path

Act upon what you know, and take precaution in what you do not know so that it becomes obvious for you, and if it does not become obvious, know that you have not acted upon some of your knowledge.

236. Persistence of Minor Sins

Some people think that we have passed the stage of refraining from sins; they are unaware of the fact that sinning is not confined to the renowned greater sins; rather, persistence of minor sins is also a greater sin.

237. Greatest Practical Dhikr

No dhikr (invocation) is greater than practical dhikr. No practical dhikr is greater than refraining from sins in acts and beliefs.

238. The Main Goal

The goal should be to spend our entire life in the remembrance of God ﷻ, His ﷻ obedience and in His ﷻ worship, in order to reach the highest degree of proximity possible for us.

239. Is it Possible?

Is it possible for our caravan to reach the destination through this dangerous path safely, without having with us the weapon of obedience of God ﷻ?

240. Reality of Spiritual Wayfaring

Q: I have decided to seek nearness to God ﷻ and have a spiritual wayfaring; what should I do?

A: In the Name of God ﷻ.If the seeker is truthful, refraining from sins is enough for all his life, even if it be a thousand years.

241. Removing Fatigue in Prayers

Q: What should one do to remove fatigue and laziness from one's prayers?

A: Busy yourselves with Mustaḥab prayers when active, and suffice yourselves with wājibāt during times of exhaustion.

242. The Fulfillment of Prayers

The condition for the fulfillment of prayers is abstinence from sins... sometimes the best interest is in delaying the response, and sometimes it is in altering the response for the better. The one who prays, thinks that his prayers have not been responded, whilst the people of certainty understand.

243. Companion

Befriend one whom, the moment you see him, you remember God ﷻ and his obedience; and do not befriend those who always think about committing sins and prevent us from remembrance of God ﷻ.

244. Self-Building in All Stages

We must know that our remedy lies in self-reform in all stages, and we shall never become needless of it, and without it, we will never reach our goal.

245. The *Malakut* of One Ṣalawāt

God ﷻ knows best the reality, spirituality, and form of one ṣalawāt that one recites and bestows upon a dead person.

246. The Reality of Tears

These (shedding of) tears was the way of all the Prophets, peace be upon them, for the delight of meeting God ﷻ, and acquiring divine pleasure. These tears of the eyes are connected to the highest of Heavens.

247. For the Fulfillment of Desires

Those who have important desires, should offer the ordinary prayers and acts of worship that have been mentioned for the fulfillment of desires, and if they want to emphasize on their need and make sure that it is fulfilled, then they should go into sajdah after their supplications and prayers and try to shed even just one tear the size of a mosquito's wing; this is a sign of the fulfillment of the desire.

248. Ascent of the Soul

Although man's soul has a clothing of soil, it is capable of soaring extraordinarily high.

249. Lack of Harmony between Knowledge and Practice

Most of our misery is because our knowledge is not in harmony with our acts!

250. Witnessing the Praising of the Entities

If man attains perfection, he would hear and witness the entities praising God ﷻ when awake.

251. The Prophet's Intimacy with the Night

In fact, Prophet Muḥammad ﷺ used to receive Divine Knowledge through his night vigils, wakefulness at dawn, and intimacy with the night... Yes, those special moments and that Divine Mercy at dawn!

252. The Persistence of *Dhikr* (Invocation)

Man should constantly be engaged in dhikr (invocation)! One, who is always engaged in dhikr, always sees himself in the presence of God ﷻ, and is in continuous discourse with God ﷻ.

253. How Should We Be?

How great it is for one to say that he hasn't done anything when he carries out a good act, or an act of worship, but when he sees others doing good, he says what a great act they have done!

254. The Source of Ethical Vices

All moral vices rise from the weakness in recognizing God عز و جل! If man understands that God عز و جل is always and in all cases more beautiful than any beauty, he will not disjoin from intimacy with God عز و جل.

255. Having Faith in God

If we trust our master only as much as a little child trusts his parents, our affairs will be solved.

256. To Believe

If we really believed in paradise and eternal prosperity, we would not oppose the divine laws this much!

257. The Consequence of Persisting in Sins

If we do not stop ourselves from committing sins, we will end up denying, belying and mocking the Divine Signs, or we may reach a point where we will become hopeless of God's عز و جل mercy.

258. Eating and Drinking

All corruption and aggression on earth, in the past, present, and future, is because of this eating and drinking, for obligations are aimed towards anger and carnal desires, whilst food and drink are its cause.

259. The Stage of Witnessing

Belief and certainty of believers has degrees, and it is possible for one to reach the stage of witnessing from the higher stages of belief, and for his certainty to increase.

260. Always and Everywhere with God

Prophets عليهم السلام dealt with God عزّ وجلّ, and wherever they would face a problem, they would turn to God عزّ وجلّ immediately. They would remember God عزّ وجلّ even during times of happiness, in a way that it was as though they would see God عزّ وجلّ as the source of everything.

261. Effect of Adhering to Infallibles' Supplications

The first stage of adhering to the supplications of Ahl al-Bayt عليهم السلام is to sit down and become familiar with them.

262. All this Greed, for What?

One who is filled with some dry bread, or he can live with vegetables, yogurt and cheese, why does he have all this greed for the world, and the wealth of this world?!

263. We do not consider Ourselves Sick

We do not consider ourselves sick; else, its treatment is easy.

264. Effects of *Ḥalāl* Food

The past scholars were so successful in gaining knowledge and acting upon it, had blessed lives, and were protected from intellectual deviations, and all this was the result of eating *Ḥalāl* food, and refraining from doubtful food.

265. Strengthening the Perception of His Presence

How should we be if we see God ﷻ present and a witness everywhere?!... In the presence of a being from whom separation is impossible, and who is present and a witness over us everywhere, how should we be and not commit sins?! The more this perception of presence strengthens, the more protected and safer man would be, and the more it weakens, the lesser his safety and protection would be.

266. Why are We not at Peace?

The verse 'Indeed hearts find rest in God's remembrance,' states that the dhikrollah (remembrance of God) is the sole cause of the hearts attaining peace and tranquility. Based on this, can we who do not have peace, claim that we remember Him?

267. Our Accounts with God

Had we settled out accounts with God ﷻ, our other accounts would also be settled.

268. We are not Concerned about Our Treatment

We know the illness, but are not concerned about its treatment. We have identified the medicine too, as the Qur'ān says, "And He inspired man with its virtues and vices," but we are not concerned about its treatment.

269. Difference in State

We regret because of having seen scholars that are very different to us (in terms of spirituality), so much so that it feels as though there is a distance of a few hundred years between us and them.

270. Modest Poor

Some are so modest that they are not willing to state their needs despite all their poverty and misery! Must neighbors and colleagues not look after such people?

271. Right Way of Inviting Towards Islam

If a Muslim intends to live in line with the Islamic Civilization, and invite others to the truth of Islam, or help Muslims remain steadfast in their faith so that they do not run away to lands of kufr (disbelief and infidelity) he must know the laws of Islam and abide by all of them.

272. Meaning of 'Life' in the Verse of the Qur'ān

God ﷻ says,

﴿وَمَن أَحياها فَكَأَنَّما أَحيَا النّاسَ جَميعًا﴾

﴾wa-man 'aḥyāhā fa ka 'annamā 'aḥyā n-nāsa jamī'an﴿

﴾and whoever saves a life is as though he had saved all mankind﴿[20]

[20] Sūrat al-Mā'idah, Verse 32.

The meaning of 'life' in this verse is rescuing from deviations and misguidance in religion.

273. Necessity of Pleading and Expressing Humility

Should we not be in a state of pleading with God ﷻ because of all these afflictions that befall the Muslims?

274. Sweet as Sookies

From the following verse, it is learnt that patience, forbearance, and hearing nonsense and accepting them like sweets is of the prerequisites of enjoining the good and forbidding evil.

﴿أَقِمِ الصَّلاةَ وَأمُر بِالمَعروفِ وَانهَ عَنِ المُنكَرِ وَاصبِر عَلى ما أَصابَكَ﴾

﴾aqimi ṣ-ṣalāta wa-'mur bi-l-ma'rūfi wa-nha 'ani l-munkari wa-ṣbir 'ala ma 'aṣabaka﴿

﴾Maintain the prayer and bid what is right and forbid what is wrong, and be patient through whatever may visit you﴿[21]

275. Retribution of Our Deeds

All afflictions occur with our own will; because we abandon the obedience of God ﷻ and choose

---

[21] Sūrat Luqmān, Verse 17.

sinning with our own desire, we inevitably face its retribution in the form of difficulties and afflictions.

276. Although We are Nothing

May we not become satisfied with ourselves. If we become pleased with ourselves, we will not be able to fulfill the rights of our Lord ﷻ in His ﷻ obedience and servitude. Although we are nothing, we consider ourselves as everything.

277. Effects of Doubtful Money

The reason behind our having fallen behind is that we spend doubtful money, and doubtful money leads to doubts and uncertainty!

278. Necessity of Self-Pessimism

Everyone should be pessimistic about, and have a negative opinion regarding his deeds, before God ﷻ as well as his own self.

279. Worry for Sustenance

May it be such that certainty becomes man's sustenance! How great it is for man to be at peace with regards to the thought of sustenance, for anxiety and worry is worse than the trouble of working. One who is afflicted with worry for his sustenance, works day and night, and is always bothered about it.

280. Need for Supplication and Seeking Intersession

During times of difficulty, and for repelling afflictions, one must not let go of supplication and seeking intercession.

281. Prayers that are Answered

He, who wants his prayers to be answered, should pray for the rescue of the believers, so that he may be included in the prayers of angels, which is definitely answered.

282. Importance of *Mustaḥab* Deeds

They are the mustaḥab deeds that get man to a (spiritual) stage!

283. They have Not asked Us to Dig a Mountain

They عليهم السلام have not asked us to dig a mountain in our worship; the most difficult part is to offer night prayers, which in reality, requires a change in our sleeping times, not an absolute lack of sleep. Rather, sleep half an hour earlier, so that you wake up half an hour earlier.

284. Necessity of Remaining Connected to the Spring

May it be such that our knowledge and maʿrifa, just like a river that is connected to the sea, remains connected to its source, even if the connection is as thin as a thread. Otherwise, even a pool full of water has no benefit, continuity, and freshness if it is not connected to the springhead.

285. Seeker of Greater Beauty

One who seeks the greater beauty is oblivious to the lower beauties.

286. Removing the Veils in Prayers

Do we need picks and spades for removing the veils?! For instance, the best way is in prayers; do we need to carry tools with us in prayers in order to combat the veils?!

287. Everything Other than God is Transient

Nothing other than God ﷿ can help us!

Tomorrow, everything other than God ﷿ shall perish.

﴿وَاللَّهُ خَيْرٌ وَأَبْقَىٰ﴾

﴿*wa-llāhu khayrun wa-'abqā*﴾

﴿*God is better and more lasting*﴾[22]

288. True Covenant

If we deviate a little from the path, the Satans among men and jinn will take over us. If one finds the path of salvation, he should be sure that this is the goal. We should make a covenant of staying in the path of God ﷻ, not intending to do wrong, and staying away from the minor sins.

289. Degrees of Jihad and Divine Guidance

Divine Guidance and Jihad of the servants, each has a degree. Each degree of Jihad and effort of the servant brings about a degree of divine guidance.

290. Steps to Progress and Success

One of the other responsibilities, along with all the other struggles, is to recite the Qur'ān in its proper manner (i.e. in the way it is worthy to be read), such that we learn something new in every recitation. We must also benefit from each of our prayers more than before,

[22] Sūrat Ṭā Ḥā, Verse 73.

rather than just repeating it in the same manner without any difference.

291. Reason and Intellect

Intellect, reason, perspicacity, and intelligence in mundane and religious affairs help earn the pleasure of God ﷻ. These understandings rescue man from the disasters of this world and the punishment of the Hereafter!

292. Useless Acts

Sometimes some individuals end up carrying out extraordinarily hard things that others are incapable of carrying out; however, it does not have any remarkable benefit for his fellow-creatures.

293. Result of Truly Recognizing this World

It is very rare for someone's life to be in line with his desires. All worldly pleasures are accompanied with numerous grievances. If one accepts and looks at the world in this way, he would become less upset because of the evils of his spouse and neighbors, for he would not expect more from this world except that it is a house of afflictions.

294. Criterion for Value

The conflict of men is in their knowledge and ignorance; and the value of men is also in their knowledge, not in their wealth.

295. Reason Behind Our Having Fallen Behind

It appears that the reason behind our having fallen behind is in our neglecting Mustaḥabbāt! Scholars of the past were committed to Mustahabbaat, such as Ziarah, Du'ā', recitation of the Qur'ān, offering prayers on time, and avoiding the Makruhaat, such as sleeping before sunrise.

296. There is a Task for Every Day

It is a loss to leave today's duties for tomorrow, for tomorrow will have its own tasks. If today passes, it shall be gone and will not be compensable.

297. *Tawfīq* is Something Completely Different

Tawfīq (divine assistance) has nothing to do with wealth, poverty, sleep, and wakefulness. It sometimes happens that one is wealthy but not successful at doing good, and sometimes even little income is full of grace and blessings.

298. Seekers of Guidance and *Ma'rifa*

If one is eager to seek guidance and ma'rifa (cognizance of God) and is serious and sincere in his demand, with the permission of God ﷻ, all of creation would become his guide.

299. For Our Supplications and Weeping

God ﷻ never sends afflictions without wisdom; rather, he sends it for us to pray and supplicate. Therefore, for relief from these, supplicating is necessary, and humility at his threshold is desirable.

300. Necessity of Moving Through the Right Path

Sometimes we do not act upon the explicit and easy commands of jurisprudence that we are already aware of, and then we go to teachers of ethics and spirituality to ask for heavy dhikrs (invocations) and matters heavier and greater than what we need... This indicates that we do not want to progress and reach perfection and higher levels of spirituality through the right path.

301. Definite Punishment

There does not exist in this world an oppression without revenge for its oppressor.

302. Beyond this World

Anyone who pays attention, and has insight, will acknowledge that there is a hidden spiritual world at work beyond this world.

303. People of Insight and *Murāqaba*

There were people who, if they committed a sin or mistake, ate impure food, they would realize and say, "We became dark, a veil has overcome us."

304. Reality of Servitude

The purpose of creation is servitude,

﴿وَما خَلَقْتُ الجِنَّ وَالإِنسَ إِلّا لِيَعْبُدونِ﴾

﴿wa-mā khalaqtu l-jinna wa-l-'insa 'illā li-ya'budūni﴾

﴿I did not create the jinn and the humans except that they may worship Me﴾[23]

and the reality of servitude is refraining from sins in belief, which is the act of the heart, and in acts of the body.

[23] Sūrat al-Dhāriyāt, Verse 56.

305. Alchemy of Prosperity

If we want our perfection, and ourselves we must be God's friend! And if we are God's friend, we must be the friend of the intermediaries of blessings from the Prophet and his progeny ﷺ. Thus, the alchemy of prosperity is the remembrance of God ﷻ, and He ﷻ is the driving force of the muscles towards the causes of absolute prosperity.

306. Abstinence from Sins Completely

Abstinence from sins is not attained such that it becomes second nature, except through muraqabah and the remembrance of God ﷻ in every state, time, place, in public and in private.

307. Stages of Love and Lovers

We love Imām al-Mahdi عجل الله تعالى فرجه الشريف since he is the Commander of the Bees. All our affairs reach us through him, and the Prophet ﷺ has appointed him as our commander. We love the Prophet ﷺ because God ﷻ has appointed him as an intercessor between God ﷻ and us, and we love God ﷻ because he is the source of all goodness, and the existence of contingent beings is His ﷻ grace.

308. Following the Intermediaries of Grace

Seeking intersession with the intermediaries of grace is carried out through its own specified mediums. We must seek their guidance and follow their leadership in order to become successful!

309. More Effective Advices

Practical preaching is higher and more effective than verbal preaching.

310. In the Path of God and the Prophet's Happiness

It is of the obvious facts that daily recitation of the Qur'ān and supplications appropriate for different times and places following prayers, and elsewhere, increased going to mosques and shrines, visiting scholars and the virtuous, and sitting down with them, all please God ﷻ and his Prophet ﷺ. We must pay more attention every day to (gaining) better insight and intimacy with worship, recitation (of the Qur'ān) and ziyāra.

311. Best ʿĪd Gift

On the blessed ʿĪds of Islam and faith, we ask God ﷻ to grant us success at our firm and continuous determination of abstaining from sins, for it is the key to prosperity in the world and hereafter.

312. Ease and Desire

If this path (servitude and abstinence of sins) was hard to the end, and did not end at ease and desire, it would not have been set up as the responsibility, and cause of encouragement, by the All-Powerful and Benevolent Creator.

313. Absolute Persistence from Sins

It appears that abstinence from sins in its absolute form (abstaining from all sins) will not take place without permanent attentive observation (murāqaba).

314. Look at the Book of Religion

Let us not look at (i.e. follow) each other; rather, look at the book of Religion, and act or abstain in accordance with it.

315. The Effect of Acting Upon Our Knowledge

One who acts upon his knowledge, God ﷻ teaches him that which he does not know!

316. Life and Death

If half of one's life is spent in remembrance of the true benefactor and the other half in ignorance, then half of his life is considered as life and the other half as death.

Allusions to the Greatness of the Noble Qur'ān

317. The Book of Reality

If there was a book that showed an image of things, then such a book is the Qur'ān that shows the image of heaven and hell.

318. The Wonders and Secrets of the Qur'ān for Believers

God ﷻ knows best what miracles the Qur'ān has for the believers, especially if they are men of knowledge, and what things they would see through it!

319. The Real Beauty of the Qur'ān

Only if we were to see the Qur'ān in its real form would it become clear if we are able to distinguish our hands from an orange.[24]

---

[24] This is in reference to the story of the women of Egypt, who cut their hands with a knife when they saw Prophet Yūsuf ﷺ.

320. The Greatest Program of Self-Development

The Qur'ān is the last program of self-development that has been placed at our disposal, but we don't appreciate it!

321. If We Would Act Upon the Qur'ān

If we would act upon the Qur'ān, we would attract others to Islam and the Qur'ān, because the Qur'ān is inclusive of all the perfections of the Ulu al-'Azm al-Anbiyā' (the resolute amongst the Prophets) عليهم السلام.

322. People are Seeking Light

If we would truly act upon the Qur'ān, we would attract others through our actions, because most people, apart from a very few, are seekers of light.

323. We Do Not Appreciate the Qur'ān and Ahl al-Bayt

Qur'ān takes man to the epitome of human perfection. We do not appreciate the Qur'ān and its equal, Ahl al-Bayt عليهم السلام.

324. Remedy for Eyes

Looking at the Qur'ān continuously is the remedy for the pain of eyes.

325. Weakness in Certainty

If we do not benefit from the Qur'ān, it is because there is weakness in our certitude.

326. Importance of Memorizing the Qur'ān

God ﷻ knows best the role of memorizing the Qur'ān in being able to derive benefit from this treasure and source of divine mercy [...] We do not benefit from the Qur'ān as we ought to!

327. Miracles of the Qur'ān

﴿وَلَو أَنَّ قُرآنًا سُيِّرَت بِهِ الجِبالُ أَو قُطِّعَت بِهِ الأَرضُ أَو كُلِّمَ بِهِ المَوتىٰ﴾

﴾wa-law 'anna qur'ānan suyyirat bihi l-jibālu 'aw quṭṭi'at bihi l-'arḍu 'aw kullima bihi l-mawtā﴿

﴾If only it were a Qur'ān[1] whereby the mountains could be moved, or the earth could be toured,[2] or the dead could be spoken to...[3]﴿[25]

What is it saying?! Are the affairs mentioned in this verse impossible and unrealistic? Or is the verse saying that the people of the Qur'ān can do all of these through the Qur'ān?!

328. Pondering Over the Qur'ān and Ḥadīth

He is acquainted with the Qur'ān who ponders more over it; the aḥādīth are just like the Qur'ān.

---

[25] Sūrat al-Ra'd, Verse 31.

1. Or 'Even if it were a Qur'ān.'
2. Or 'the ground could be split,' i.e., for making springs and wells.
3. Ellipsis. The phrase omitted is 'all unbelievers would have embraced the faith.' Or 'still they would not have embraced the faith.' Cf. 6:111.

329. What Need is there for Another Weapon?

If we are right in saying that the Qur'ān is a weapon, then what need do we have for another weapon!

330. An Existence from the Realm of Light

Do we have the faintest idea that the Qur'ān is not like other writings! It is as though the Qur'ān is a Divine Existence from the realm of light and spirituality, and has appeared in the corporeal realm.

331. Looking at the Qur'ān

We must have absolute certainty in the fact that looking at the Qur'ān is not like looking at any other book!

332. A Blessing of this Greatness

No nation has been blessed with such a Qur'ān that has all these distinctions and effects! A blessing of this greatness has been bestowed upon us, but it is as though they have not granted us (anything), and as though this book is not complementary to man!

333. Salvation of the Common People and the Elite

Tawassul (seeking intersession) with the Qur'ān, carrying, understanding, and reciting it, is beneficial for the salvation of even the common public, let alone the elite!

334. We are Culpable with Regards to the Qur'ān

It's a wonder that so much attention is paid to personalities and their words, and that their speeches are recorded, whilst the Qur'ān, which is in our hands, does not hold such value before us! We all are aware that we are culpable with regards to the Qur'ān.

335. In Search of the Wonders of the Qur'ān

One who follows the fact that Qur'ān is, 'a clarification of all things,' shall see strange and unusual (things).

336. A Book that can Train Prophets

Qur'ān is a book that can train Prophets, for Prophets are of two kinds:

Those that are designated to Prophethood by God,

And the 'Prophets of Perfection' that acquire the perfections of the prophets as a result of their beliefs, and acting upon the commands of the Qur'ān. Based on this, the Qur'ān trains prophets of perfection.

337. Striving to Study the Qur'ān and Act Upon It

We have the responsibility of striving to learn, teach, recite, and act upon the Qur'ān. However, whilst we place the Qur'ān upon our heads on the nights of vigil [i.e. the Nights of Power], in practice, we step upon the verses of hijab, backbiting, lying and the verses,

﴿وَيلٌ لِلمُطَفِّفينَ﴾

﴾waylun li-l-muṭaffifīna﴿

﴾Woe to the defrauders who use short measures﴿[26]

﴿وَقَضىٰ رَبُّكَ أَلّا تَعبُدوا إِلّا إِيّاهُ وَبِالوالِدَينِ إِحسانًا ۚ إِمّا يَبلُغَنَّ عِندَكَ الكِبَرَ أَحَدُهُما أَو كِلاهُما فَلا تَقُل لَهُما أُفٍّ وَلا تَنهَرهُما وَقُل لَهُما قَولًا كَريمًا﴾

﴾wa-qaḍā rabbuka 'allā ta'budū 'illā 'iyyāhu wa-bi-l-wālidayni 'iḥsānan 'immā yablughanna 'indaka l-kibara 'aḥaduhumā 'aw kilāhumā fa-lā taqul lahumā 'uffin wa-lā tanharhumā wa-qul lahumā qawlan karīman﴿

[26] Sūrat al-Muṭaffifīn, Verse 1.

﴾*Your Lord has decreed that you shall not worship anyone except Him, and [He has enjoined] kindness to parents. Should they reach old age at your side —one of them or both — do not say to them, 'Fie!'*[1] *And do not chide them, but speak to them noble words*﴿[27]

and

﴿وَلَا تَمْشِ فِي الْأَرْضِ مَرَحًا﴾

﴾*wa-lā tamshi fī l-'arḍi maraḥan*﴿

﴾*Do not walk exultantly on the earth*﴿[28]

Spiritual Instructions

338. Always and Everywhere

The supplications reported for specific places and times are not restricted such that they cannot be recited at other places or times; in fact, these instructions are desirable in multiplicity.

---

[27] Sūrat al-Isrā', Verse 23.

1. That is, do not grumble or speak to them in an ill-tempered manner. *Uff* is an interjection expressing displeasure and exasperation, indicating that one has been put out of patience.

[28] Sūrat al-Isrā', Verse 37.

339. The Etiquettes and Conditions of Supplication

Supplication requires the following:

1. Praising the Almighty God ﷻ

2. Confessing to one's sins and being penitent for them, which is just like repentance or the consequence of it.

3. Sending ṣalawāt (peace and blessings) upon Prophet Muḥammad and his descendants عليهم السلام, who are the intermediaries of Divine Grace.

4. Weeping, and if that is not possible, pretending to cry, although it may be very brief.

5. And after all of these, seek one's desires, which in this case, will be fulfilled. Of course, it is better if all these are done in sajdah (prostration).

340. For the Health of Eyes

In order to keep one's eyes healthy, Āyat Al-Kursī should be recited after prayers, following which, one must put his hands on his eyes and say, "Allāhumma iḥfaz hadaqatayya biḥaqqi hadaqatay 'Alī b. Abi Ṭālib Amīr al-Mu'minīn 'alayhi as-salām." (O God, protect my two eyes for the sake of the two eyes of 'Alī b. Abī

Ṭālib, the Commander of the Faithful, peace be upon him!)

341. For Curing the Sick

For curing the sick, the Water of Zamzam and the soil of Karbalā should be given to him several times, Sadaqah should be given several times to different people, even if the value is not much; Sūrat al-Fātiḥah should be recited between one to hundred times by different people. These are very effective. In addition to these, the ill person must ask his friends to pray for him.

342. In Order to Remain Safe

In order to remain safe, recite the following three times every morning and evening:

"Allāhuma ijʿal fī dirʿika al-hasīnati allatī tajʿalu fīhā man turīdu."

(O God, keep me in your strong, protective armor wherein you keep those whom you intend to!)

343. Finding the Lost

For finding the lost or stolen things, even if it may be a person, recite this dhikr a lot: "Asbahtu fī amānillah, amsaytu fī jawārillah." (I started my day in the protection of God, my night began in the protection of God).

344. For the Increase in Sustenance

One who wants an increase in his sustenance should recite the following dhikr a lot, with a ṣalawāt in the beginning and end: "Allahumma aghninī bihalālika ʻan ḥarāmika wa bifaḍlika ʻan man siwāk." (O God, make me needless of your harām (unlawful) through your halāl (lawful), and from all other than you through your bounties and mercy.)

345. Getting Rid of Pretentiousness of Virtue

Q: What should I do to get rid of the pretentiousness of virtue?

A: You should repeatedly recite the ḥawqala with full belief in it, i.e. recite repeatedly "Lā ḥawla walā quwwata illā billāh (There is no power or strength except through God).

346. The Remedy for Anger

Q: What should we do to cure anger?

A: Recite ṣalawāt repeatedly with full belief, "A llāhumma Ṣalli ʻalā Muhammadin wa ʻalā āli Muḥammad."

347. The Remedy for Pride

Q: What way would you recommend for curing pride?

A: In the Name of the Most High—Reciting ḥawqala (Lā ḥawla walā quwwata illā billāh—There is no power or strength except through God) repeatedly is the remedy for pride.

348. Curing Scrupulosity

Q: I am very scrupulous; please guide me in curing it!

A: Repeating Tahlīl (Lā Ilāha Illallāh – there is no god but God) is the remedy for scrupulosity.

349. In Plights and Afflictions

In plights and afflictions, this is the best dhikr (invocation) that we have received from the Prophet ﷺ, "La ḥawla walā quwwata illā billāh al-ʿAlī al-ʿāzīm, lā malja'a walā manja'a min Allāhi illā ilayh."

350. For the Repelling of Afflictions

For the repelling of afflictions, this supplication is also useful: "Allāhumma Ṣali ʿalā Muḥammad wa ʿalā āli Muḥammad wa amsik ʿannā al-sūʾ."

(O God, send blessings on Muḥammad and his descendants and keep evils aloof from us!)

351. Sincerity of Intention in Work and Worship

Q: How should we not forget the sincerity of our intention in all our works and worship?

A: In the Name of the Most High – Do not give way to anything other than God ﷻ and His remembrance in all your acts and worship; this is the exclusive path to salvation!

352. For Concentration of the Mind

Q: What should we do in order to increase the concentration of the mind?

A: Recite repeatedly the dhikrs (invocations) that are effective in mental clarity, such as 'Lā Ilāha Illallāh.'

353. Resolving Conflicts in Marriage

Q: What should couples that have conflicts in their married lives do?

A: The one who seeks to bring the conflicts to an end or anyone else should give ṣadaqa repeatedly to different people and pray much for reconciliation between the two.

A Spiritual Instruction from Āyatullāh Bahjat

In the Name of God, the Beneficent, the Merciful

All praises belong to God , the Lord of all the worlds, and blessings be on the leader of the Messengers and Prophets and on his progeny ﷺ, the leaders of the pure successors, and on all the infallibles, and continuous curses be on all their enemies.

A group of people seeks advice and counsel from this nondescript. If it is desired that we speak and they listen, and once again at another time, we speak and they listen, then it is not hidden from those who know that this insignificant being is incapable of doing so. And if they say that they want a word that would be the 'mother of all words' and suffice for absolute prosperity in both worlds, then God ﷻ is capable of bringing out such a word from the words of this insignificant being and make it reach you.

The purpose of creation is servitude:

﴿وَما خَلَقْتُ الجِنَّ وَالإِنسَ إِلّا لِيَعْبُدونِ﴾

﴾*wa-mā khalaqtu l-jinna wa-l-ʾinsa ʾillā li-yaʿbudūni*﴿

﴾*I did not create the jinn and the humans except that they may worship Me*﴿[29]

[29] Sūrat al-Dhāriyāt, Verse 56.

And the reality of servitude is abstinence from committing sins in beliefs, which are the acts of the heart, and in the physical acts. And abstinence from sins is not achieved to the point where it becomes one's second nature, except through constant self-watchfulness and remembrance of God in all states, times and places, whilst alone and in public: "And I do not say Subhan God and Alhamdu lillah, rather, it is the remembrance of God before his obligations and prohibitions."

We love the Imām of the time عجل الله تعالى فرجه الشريف because he is like the queen bee. All our affairs reach us through him عجل الله تعالى فرجه الشريف without exceptions, and the Messenger ﷺ has appointed him عجل الله تعالى فرجه الشريف as our leader, and we love the Messenger because God ﷻ has established him as the intermediary between us and Him ﷻ, and we love God ﷻ because He ﷻ is the source of all good and the existence of contingent beings is His ﷻ grace. Thus, if we like ourselves, and perfection for ourselves, we must befriend God ﷻ, and if we are His ﷻ friend, we must befriend the intermediaries of His ﷻ Grace from the prophets and successors, or else, we either do not love our own selves, or we do not love the Bestower of Gifs, or we do not love the intermediaries of His ﷻ Grace.

Thus, the elixir of prosperity is the remembrance of God ﷻ, and He ﷻ is the mover of our body parts towards the causes of absolute prosperity. Seeking intercession of the intermediaries is benefitting from the source of all good, through intermediaries appointed by Himself. We must follow their guidance and step on their footsteps under their leadership in order to become successful.

Do not seek further explanation, record that which was said, and embed it in your hearts and it will be self-explanatory. If you ask why I do not act upon this myself, we will say, "If it was decided that we must say that we act in accordance to all that we know, perhaps we would not have become ready for being present and this discourse." However, the instruction is the spreading of blessings, and perhaps it may be in accordance with what is desired, "God has not made it obligatory on the servants to learn till He has made it obligatory on the learned to teach."[30]

Let it also be known that if it becomes possible for anybody, practical counsel is greater than verbal counsel is, "Be the callers towards God without your tongues."[31]

May God ﷻ help you and us succeed in that which pleases Him and may He keep us away from all that which earns His wrath. Peace, mercy and blessings of God ﷻ be upon you. All praises belong to God ﷻ, in the

[30] Sharīf Raḍī, Muḥammad b. al-Ḥusayn, *Nahj al-Balāgha*, Saying 478.

[31] Kulaynī, Shaykh Muḥammad b. Yaʿqūb, *al-Kāfī*, Vol. 2, p. 78.

beginning and end. Blessings be on Muḥammad and his pure progeny and curses be on all their enemies.

Mashhad

Rabīʿ ath-Thānī

1420 AH (July 1999)

The Blessed Du'ā'

As the late Āyatullāh said (short saying #45), recite specifically this blessed Du'ā' and ask God ﷻ to bring us the Possessor of Affairs عجل الله تعالى فرجه الشريف

دعاء عظم البلاء وبرح الخفاء

Du'ā' 'Aẓumal-Bala' wa Bariḥal-Khafa'

اِلٰهي عَظُمَ الْبَلاءُ

Ilāhī, 'aẓumal balā',

My God, my afflictions have become enormous,

وَبَرِحَ الْخَفاءُ

wa bariḥal khafā',

the matter has come out,

وَانْكَشَفَ الْغِطاءُ

wan kashafal ghiṭā',

the veil has been lifted,

وَانْقَطَعَ الرَّجاءُ

wan qaṭaʿar rajāʾ,

hope has been cut off,

وَضاقَتِ الأَرْضُ

wa ḍāqatil arḍu,

the earth has become narrow [despite its expanse],

وَمُنِعَتِ السَّماءُ

wa muniʿatis samāʾ,

and the heaven's mercy has been withheld,

وأَنْتَ الْمُسْتَعانُ

wa antal mustaʿānu,

and You are my resort,

وَإِلَيْكَ الْمُشْتَكى

wa ilaykal mushtakā,

and to You I bring my complaint,

وَعَلَيْكَ الْمُعَوَّلُ فِي الشِّدَّةِ والرَّخاءِ

Wa ʿalaykal muʿawwalu fish shiddati war rakhāʾ!

and on You is my reliance in distress and ease.

اَللّٰهُمَّ صَلِّ عَلى مُحَمَّد وَآلِ مُحَمَّد

Allāhumma, ṣalli ʿalā Muḥammadin wa āli Muḥammad,

O God, bless Muḥammad and the Family of Muḥammad,

أُولِي الأَمْرِ الَّذينَ فَرَضْتَ عَلَيْنا طاعَتَهُمْ

ūlil amr, alladhīna faraḍta ʿalaynā ṭāʿatahum,

whom You have invested with the authority to command,

وَعَرَّفْتَنا بِذلِكَ مَنْزِلَتَهُمْ

wa ʿarraftanā bi dhālika manzilatahum,

and enjoined us to obey,

فَفَرِّجْ عَنا بِحَقِّهِمْ فَرَجاً عاجِلاً قَرِيباً كَلَمْحِ الْبَصَرِ اَوْ هُوَ اَقْرَبُ

fa farrij 'annā bi ḥaqqihim farajan 'ājilan, qarīban, ka lamḥil baṣari aw huwa aqrab.

So grant us relief, for their sake, a relief that is early and prompt, like the twinkling of the eye or even quicker!

يا مُحَمَّدُ يا عَلِيُّ يا عَلِيُّ يا مُحَمَّدُ

Yā Muḥammadu yā 'Alī, yā 'Alīyu yā Muḥammad,

O Muḥammad! O 'Alī! O 'Alī! O Muḥammad!

اِكْفِياني فَاِنَّكُما كافِيانِ

ikfiyānī fa innakumā kāfiyān,

Suffice me! For you are indeed my sufficers.

وَانْصُراني فَاِنَّكُما ناصِرانِ

wanṣurānī fa innakumā nāṣirān!

And help me! For indeed you are my helpers.

يا مَوْلانا يا صاحِبَ الزَّمانِ

Yā mawlānā, yā Ṣāḥibaz Zamān,

O our master, Master of the Era!

الْغَوْثَ الْغَوْثَ الْغَوْث

alghawth, alghawth, alghawth!

Help me! Help me! Help me!

اَدْرِكْني اَدْرِكْني اَدْرِكْني

Adriknī, adriknī, adriknī!

Rescue me! Rescue me! Rescue me!

السّاعَةَ السّاعَةَ السّاعَةَ

Assā'ata, assā'ata, assā'ah!

This hour! This hour! This hour!

الْعَجَلَ الْعَجَلَ الْعَجَل

Al'ajal, al'ajal, al'ajal!

Make haste! Make haste! Make haste!

يا أَرْحَمَ الرّاحِمِينَ

Yā arḥamar rāḥimīn,

O Most Merciful of the merciful,

بِحَقِّ مُحَمَّد وَآلِهِ الطّاهِرِينَ

bi ḥaqqi Muhammadin wa ālihiṭ ṭāhirīn!

For the sake of Muḥammad and his immaculate Family!

www.ingramcontent.com/pod-product-compliance
Lightning Source LLC
Chambersburg PA
CBHW071149120626
46546CB00006B/2188
* 9 7 8 1 9 5 6 2 7 6 3 1 2 *